"*Thy worst! I fart at thee.*"

-Ben Jonson, *The Alchemist (i,I)*

Fee! Fie! Foe! Fum!

A Dictionary Of Fartology

By

Professor E. Slove Promblès

PUBLISHED BY MELODIOUS PUBLICATIONS
Post Office Box 343
Brockport, New York   14420

"An area seared by the Flames of Revivalism"

Library of Congress Cataloging in Publication Data

Promblés, E. Slove.
    Fee, fie, foe, fum.

    Bibliography: p. 128
    1. Flatulence--Anecdotes, facetiae, satire, etc
I. Title.   II. Title: Fartology.
PN6231.F55P7   818'.5402   81-16845
ISBN 0-941086-00-3   AACR2

First Printing September 1981

Printed in the United States of America

ISBN 0-941086-00-3

All correspondence sent to Melodious Publications will be treated as unconditionally assigned for publication. Upon receipt these items will become the exclusive property of Melodious Publications and as such are subject to Melodious Publications' unrestricted right to edit and comment editorially and artistically.

ACKNOWLEDGMENTS

Melodious Publications wishes to thank the following for allowing permission to quote from...

Carol Belanger Grafton's *Bizarre & Ornamental Alphabets;* 1981, Dover Publications, Inc. (This is where I got the large fancy letters from.)

R.S. Rattray's *Ashanti Law and Constitution* by permission of Oxford University Press.

Carl Sagan's *The Cosmic Connection* by permission of Doubleday & Co., Inc.

John Barth's *The Floating Opera* by permission of Doubleday & Co., Inc.

"10 Beans and their Flatulence levels" from *The Book of Lists* by David Wallechinsky, Irving Wallace and Amy Wallace. Copyright © 1977 by David Wallechinsky, Irving Wallace and Amy Wallace. By permission of William Morrow & Co.

Theodor Rosebury's *Life on Man.* Copyright © 1969 by Theodor Rosebury. By permission of Viking Penguin, Inc.

The Unspeakable Confessions of Salvador Dali, as told to André Parinaud. English translation Copyright © 1976 by William Morrow and Company, Inc. By permission of the publishers.

A Dictionary of Slang and Unconventional English, 7th Edn., by Eric Partridge (Copyright © 1970 by Eric Partridge) By permission of MacMillan Publishing Co., Inc. and Routledge & Kegan Paul, Ltd.

The Complete Works of George Gascoigne, edited by John W. Cunliffe, II. By permission of Cambridge University Press.

R.H. Blyth's *Oriental Humour* by permission of the Hokuseido Press, © 1959, by R.H. Blyth.

Isaac Asimov's Treasury of Humor by Isaac Asimov Copyright © 1971 by Isaac Asimov. Reprinted by permission of Houghton Mifflin Company and Vallentine, Mitchell & Co. Ltd.

And of course, thank you to everyone who has ever taught me new things of which I could never have imagined or dreamt on my own:

Wayne Alber, Petrinella Chierchio, Peggy & Dick Pennington, Max Robertson, Gary Shore, Lou Katz, hitchhikers, Paula Silvestrone, Phil Ferrara, Shirley Richardson, Lena, librarians, Roger Weiss, Linda Lydle, Crazy Taysie, Christopher Flowers and definitely Ed Rubin.

This work is dedicated to the fartological endeavors of Robert, Roy and James Patterson. Fart be with them!

REALLY, this is a book in which I transform farts into indexes or fists that point the way towards some marvelous book that should be as familiar as Tom Sawyer, as familiar as Hamlet, as familiar as language (some more than others, but "what can I say?"). I like books, and this is none other than a book about books - *other* books.

I think that the word "fart" strikes deep/low/ savage enough - complete with all its psychological realms - to break a hole in the side of your head to, in turn, release some of the pressure and allow you to *think* again about something - anything. And farting is as good a thing to think about as any other thing and, glory be to farts!, there are *no experts* on the subject - not a single one! No one to intimidate you and no one to tell you - "No, you are wrong!" And unless that person shows you some pretty good proof - shows you in a way that's simple and doesn't leave you with any questions unanswered (never an easy task - even if you're right, 'cause there's always some bastard out there tellin' you *you're* wrong!) you are only left with two alternatives. In one, you say, "Yes, I am wrong and you are right because of the dif- ference of our statures; I'm smaller." The other choice is to say, "I am Truth. I am Right." Can we really deal with either of these? Both are insanity. But I claim a third way and I propose to divulge a secret door to lead you to the free- dom of Think City by just relaxing enough to sit back a minute and to think of where you are: house city country continent planet galaxy uni- verse hyperuniverse as far as you can go; and then close your eyes and travel through again. After you are done with this you'll find (at least *I* usually do) that you're probably up to starting that book you've been meaning to read. No?

A Dictionary of Fartology

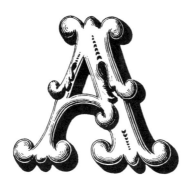

AEOLUS

As "King of the Winds" the Greek god Aeolus ruled over the four lesser gods Boreas (north wind), Zephyr (west wind), Notus (south wind) and Eurus (east wind). His home was the island of Aeolia. (24)

AEROPHAGE

This is merely the medical term for *air swallowing*. It has not a great deal of interest for fartology, but in the new and quickly developing science of *Eructology* (see ERUCTATE) it becomes essential, otherwise "burping" or "belching" cannot occur. This and the few other words taken from the eructologist's jargon are included in our study because of their obvious relatedness. (34&41:pg.165)

ARABIAN NIGHTS

Amongst 1001 Arabian nights, we find crepitus creeping conspicuously into only three of them. Stories that will never die, the three tales printed here (#408 contains only the relevant parts) are completed with club leader/editor Sir Richard Burton's elucidating comments.

JA'AFAR THE BARMECIDE AND THE OLD BADAWI
Night #395.

The Commander of the Faithful, Harun al-Rachid, went out one day, with Abu Ya'Kub the cup-companion and Ja'afar the Barmecide, and Abu Nowas, into the desert, where they fell in with an old man, propt against his ass. The Caliph bade Ja'afar learn of him whence he come; so he asked him, "Whence comest thou?" and he answered, "From Bassorah." Quoth Ja'afar, "And what wilt thou do there?" and the old man replied, "I go to seek medicine for my eye." Said the Caliph, "O Ja'afar, make thou sport with him," and answered Ja'afar, "I shall hear what I shall exceedingly mislike." But Al-Rashid rejoined, "I charge thee on my authority, jest with him." Thereupon Ja'afar said to the Badawi, "If I prescribe thee a medicine that shall profit thee, what wilt thou give me in return?" Quoth the other, "Allah Almighty will requite the kindness with what is better for thee than any requital of mine." Continued Ja'afar, "Now lend me an ear and I will give thee a prescription, which I have given to none but thee." "What is that?" asked the Badawi; and Ja'afar answered, "Take three ounces of wind-breaths and the like of sunbeams and the same of moonshine and as much of lamp-light; mix them well together and let them lie in the wind three months. Then place them three months in a mortar without a bottom and pound them to fine powder and after trituration set them in a cleft platter, and let it stand in the wind another three months; after which use of this medicine three drachms every night in thy sleep, and, Inshallah! thou shalt

2

be healed and whole." Now when the Badawi
heard this, he stretched himself out to full
length on the donkey's back and let fly a
terrible loud fart and said to Ja'afar, "Take
this fart in payment of thy prescription. When
I have followed it, if Allah grant me recovery,
I will give thee a slave-girl, who shall serve
thee in thy lifetime a service, wherewith Allah
shall cut short thy term; and when thou diest
and the Lord hurrieth thy soul to hell fire,
she shall blacken thy face with her skite, of
her mourning for thee, and shall keen and beat
her face, saying, 'O frosty-beard, what a fool
thou wast?'" Thereupon Harun al-Rashid laughed
till he fell backward, and ordered the Badawi
three thousand silver pieces.

Of the fart, Burton had the following comment to make:

"The answer is as old as the hills, *teste* the
tale of what happened when Amasis (who on horse-
back) raised his leg, 'broke wind and bade the
messenger carry it back to Apries.' *Herod. ii.*,
162. But for the full significance of the Badawi's most insulting reply see the *Tale of Abu
Hasan* in Night #410."

And here is a scene occurring in the story
of the 408th night in which...

When the Bhang-eater joined the masons he saw
the Sultan and Wazir overseeing them; and, as
soon as the King sighted him, he opened his
breast to him and said, "O man, wilt thou also
do work?" and said the other, "Yes." So he bade
him labour with the builders and he continued
toiling till hard upon noontide, at which time
he remembered his slave-girl and forthright he
bowed his head upon his bosom-pocket and he
sniffed thereat. The Wazir saw him so doing and
asked him "What is the meaning of thy sniffing
at what is in thy poke?" and he answered, "No
matter." However the Minister expied him a second time occupied in like guise and quoth he
to the Sultan, "Look, O King of the Age, at your

3

labourer who is hiding something in his pocket and smelling thereat." "Haply," responded the Sultan, "there is in his pouch something he would look at." However when the Sultan"s glance happened to fall that way he beheld the Bhangeater sniffing and smelling at his poke, so he said to the Wazir, "Wallahi! Verily this workman's case is a strange one." Hereupon both fixed their eyes upon him and they saw him again hiding somewhat in his pouch and smelling at it. The Wazir cried, "Verily this fellow is a-fizzling and he boweth his head toward his breast in order that he may savour his own fart." The Sultan laughed and said, "By Allah, if he go on this way 'tis a somewhat curious matter, or perhaps, O Wazir, he have some cause to account for it; at any rate do thou call out to him and ask him." So the Wazir arose and drawing near to him asked him saying, "Ho, this one! every time thou fizzles thou smellest and sniffest at thy fizzlings;" whereat answered the workman, "Wag not thy tongue with these words seeing thou art in the presence of a King glorious of degree." Quoth the Minister, "What is the matter with thee in this case that thou art sniffing at thy pocket?" and quoth the labourer
....

And if you are truly interested in his answer you'll have to find the story in your local library. At the story's end quoth Danyazad, "How sweet is thy story, O sister mine, and how enjoyable and delectable!"
Burton added this footnote:

"Alluding to the curious phenomenon pithily expressed in the Latin proverb, *"Suus cuique crepitus bene olet,"* I know of no exception to the rule, except amongst travelers in Tibet, where the wild onion, the only procurable greenstuff, produces an odour so rank and fetid that men run away from their own crepitations. The subject is not savoury, yet it has been copiously illustrated: I once dined at a London house whose nameless owner, a noted bibliophile, especially of *'facetiae,'* had placed upon the drawing room table a dozen books treating of the *'Crepitus ventris.'* When the guests came up and drew near the table, and opened the volumes, their faces were a study. For the Arab: *'Faswah'* = a silent break wind. It is opposed to *'Zirt'* = a loud fart and the vulgar term."

HOW ABU HASAN BRAKE WIND.

Night #410.

They recount that in the City Kaukaban of Al-Yaman there was a man of the Fazli tribe who had left Badawi life, and become a townsman for many years and was a merchant of the most opulent merchants. His wife had deceased when both were young; and his friends were instant with him to marry again, ever quoting to him the words of the poet,

"Go gossip! re-wed thee, for Prime draweth near:
A wife is an almanac - good for the year."

So being weary of contention, Abu Hasan entered into negotiations with the old women who procure matches, and married a maid like Canopus when he hangeth over the seas of Al-Hind. He made high festival therefor, bidding to the wedding-banquet kith and kin, Olema and Fakirs; friends and foes and all his acquaintances of that country-side. The whole house was thrown open to feasting: there were rices of five several colours, and sherbets of as many more; and kids stuffed with walnuts and almonds and pistachios and a camel-colt roasted whole. So they ate and drank and made mirth and merriment; and the bride was displayed in her seven dresses and one more, to the women, who could not take their eyes off her. At last, the bridegroom was summoned to the chamber where she stay enthroned; and he rose slowly and with dignity from his divan; but in so doing, for that he was over full of meat and drink, lo and behold! he let fly a fart, great and terrible. Thereupon each guest turned to his neighbor and talked aloud and made as though he had heard nothing,

5

fearing for his life. But a consuming fire was
lit in Abu Hasan's heart; so he pretended a call
of nature; and in lieu of seeking the bride-cham-
ber, he went down to the house-court and saddled
his mare and rode off, weeping bitterly, through
the shadow of the night. In time he reached La-
hej where he found a ship ready to sail for India; so he slipped on board and made Calicut of
Malabar. Here he met with many Arabs, expecially
Hazramis, who recommended him to the King; and
this King (who was a Fakir) trusted him and ad-
vanced him to the captainship of his body-guard.
He remained ten years in all solace and delight
of life; at the end of which time he was seized
with home-sickness; and the longing to behold
his native land was that of a lover pining for
his beloved; and he came near to die of yearning desire. But his appointed day had not dawn-
ed; so, after taking the first bath of health,
he left the King without leave, and in due
course landed at Makalla of Hazramaut. Here he
donned the rags of a religious man; and, keeping
his name and case secret, fared for Kaukaban
a-foot; enduring a thousand hardships of hunger,
thirst and fatigue; and braving a thousand dan-
gers from the lion, the snake and the Ghul. But
when he drew near his old home, he looked down
upon it from the hills with brimming eyes, and
said in himself, "Haply they might know thee;
so I will wander about the outskirts, and heark-
en to the folk. Allah grant that my case not be
remembered by them!" He listened carefully for
seven nights and seven days, till it so chanced
that, as he was sitting at the door of a hut,
he heard the voice of a young girl saying, "O
my mother, tell me the day when I was born; for
such an one of my companions is about to take an
omen for me" and the mother answered, "Thou was
born, O my daughter, on the very night when Abu
Hasan farted." Now the listener no sooner heard
these words than he rose up from the bench, and
fled away saying to himself, "Verily thy fart
hath become a date, which shall last for ever
and ever; even as the poet said,

'As long as palms shall shift the flower;
As long as palms sift the flour.'"

And he ceased not travelling and voyaging and
returned to India; and there abode in self-exile
till he died; and the mercy of Allah be upon
him!

  Burton comments:

  "This story is curious and ethnologically val-
uable. The Badawi who eructates as a civility,
has a mortal hatred to a *crepitus ventris;* and
were a by-stander to laugh at its accidental
occurrence, he would at once be cut down as a
"pindonor." The same is the custom amongst the
Highlanders of Afghanistan, and its artificial
nature suggests direct derivation; for the two
regions are separated by a host of tribes, Per-
sians and Baloch, Sindis and Europeans. The raid
of the pre-Islamitic Arabs, over the lands lying
to the north-east of them are almost forgotten;
still there are traces, and this may be one of
them." (All stories and comments:11)

ARISTOPHANES

  Aristophanes (b. 445 BC), the early Greek
dramatist who innovated the art by using satire,
had no qualms about making the wisdom of Socrates look like "farts in a gale wind." Actually, his use of Socrates' name was an (inac-
curate?) symbol for the Sophistical logic then
developing in Athens. And Aristophanes' play
The Clouds (423 BC) was an attck on this logic.
  Within, a student of Socrates wishes to prove
his teacher's greatness:

STUDENT: You haven't heard *anything* yet. Would
    you like another example?

STREPSIADES: Oh, I'd *like* that. Go on.

STUDENT: Well, it seems that Chairephon was
    asking Sokrates which of two theories he
    held: that gnats tootled through their mouths

7

or, in reverse, through their tails.

STREPSIADES: *(eagerly)*: Gosh. Go on. What was his theory about the gnat?

STUDENT: Attend. According to him, the intestinal tract of the gnat is of puny proportions, and through this diminutive duct the gastric gas of the gnat is forced under pressure down to the rump. At that point the compressed gases, as through a narrow valve, escape with a whoosh, thereby causing the characteristic tootle or cry of the flatulent gnat.

STREPSIADES: So the gnat has a bugle up its ass! O thrice-blessed mortals! What bowel-wisdom! Why, the man who has mastered the ass of the gnat could win an acquittal from any court! (2:pg.19)

And when done extolling the farting gnat the student goes on to tell of Socrates' bad luck for which the undinist can explore for his own pleasure.

Later, to explain from whence the sound of thunder comes, we are told:

SOKRATES: The Clouds are water-packed; they collide with each other and explode because of the pressure.

STREPSIADES: Yeah? And what's your proof for that?

SOKRATES: Why, take yourself as example. You know that meat-stew the vendors sell at the Panathenaia? How it gives you the cramps and your stomach starts to rumble?

STREPSIADES: Yes, by Apollo! I remember. What an awful feeling! You feel sick and your belly churns and the fart rips loose like thunder. First just a gurgle, *pappapax;* then louder, *pappaPAPAXapaX,* and finally like thunder, *PAPAPAPAXAPAXAPPAPAXapap!*

SOKRATES: Precisely. First think of the tiny

fart that your intestines make. Then consider the heavens: their infinite farting
is thunder. For thunder and farting are, in
principle, one and the same. (2:pg.35)

ART (of Smell)

See EABOS, EDWARD R.

ASHANTI

Farting is known to cause embarrassment yet
the embarrassment of this natural function a-
mong the Ashanti tribe of African natives is
so great that death is the only honor left to
the farter. Capt. R.S. Rattray furnishes us
with an example:

During the visit of a person of considerable
importance, who was much beloved by the loyal
and generous-hearted Ashanti, the Chief and
Elders of a romote province, in common with
many others, had come to do him honour. When it
came to the turn of a certain old man to be presented, in bending forward to do obeisance, he,
unnoticed by all but his immediate followers,
inadvertantly broke wind. Within an hour of the
termination of the ceremony he had gone and
hanged himself. He had "disgraced" himself and
his following. The universal comment in Ashanti
among his fellow countrymen was that he had done
the only right thing under the circumstances.
He could never have lived down the ridicule which
he might otherwise have incurred. *Fadie ene
ewuo a, fanyinam ewuo* ("If it be a choice between disgrace and death, then death is pre-
ferable"). It was, in fact, this occasion which
first made me familiar with a proverb which I
later found to be universally known in Ashanti.
To break wind *(ata)* in public was, in Ashanti,
considered a disgraceful act. Their traditions
record several cases not unlike the above-men-

tioned more modern example. One of such was
the occasion on which a priestess of a Tano
god from B. was dancing. She came forward during the dance to kneel before Chief K.D. of M.,
and in doing so broke wind. She was seized; her
head was shaved; drums were beaten over her head
to drive away the spirit of her god; she was
driven out of the priesthood, and made to give
sheep to purify the temple of god and the "pal-
ace" of the Chief. Again, if a number of Ashanti
happened to be eating together, and one broke
wind, "the bowl of food would be placed upon
that person's head that he might be used as a
table; but," added my informant, "if the man
were among friends and was well liked, the rest
of the party might cover their mouths with
their hands and go outside that he might not
see their laughter, because they might fear
that the man who had offended would go away and
hang himself, should he notice that the others
were laughing at him." (40)

ASTOMI

There lives near the source of the river Gan-
ges a nation of people called Astomi. "They
have no mouths; their bodies are rough and hairy,
and they cover themselves with a down of either
silk or cotton plucked from the leaves of trees.
These people subsist only by breathing and by
the odours which they inhale through the nos-
trils. They support themselves upon neither
meat nor drink; when they go upon a long jour-
ney they only carry with them various odoriferous roots and flowers, and wild apples, that
they may not be without something to smell at.
But," tells us Pliny, "an odour, which is a
little more powerful than usual, easily de-
stroys them." (20&35b:pg.131-2)

"Both subtly and profoundly, the activities of life have affected the environment of our planet," tells us Carl Sagan, eminent American astronomer. And happily, he furnishes us with an example which helps establish the universality of the emerging science of fartology. For a mere fart may someday have to do away with "mereness" as our population and its survival needs expand.

"There seems to be a debate in the ecological literature on two possible sources of the methane. One source is methane bacteria, which live in swamps and marshes - hence the term "marsh gas" to refer to methane. The principal other habitat of methane bacteria is in the rumens of ungulates. There is at least one school of ecological thought that believes that more methane is produced from the latter source than the former. This means that bovine flatulence - the intimate intestinal activities of cows, reindeer, elephants and elk - is detectable over interplanetary distances, while the bulk of the activities of mankind are invisible. We would not ordinarily consider the flatulence of cattle as a dominant manifestation of life on earth, but there it is." (41a)

BARTH, JOHN (1930-   )

John Barth is one of America's great contemporary writers. Upon reading his works it became clear to me that his knowledge and exploration in fartology was not lacking. Two quotes from his first novel, *The Floating Opera*, illustrate his artistic insights into the fartician's concern.

"Olfactory pleasures being no more absolute than any other kinds of pleasures, one would do well to outgrow conventional odor-judgements, for a vast number of worthwhile smells await the unbiased nose. It is a meager standard that will call perverse that seeker of wisdom who, his toenails plucked, must sniff his fingers in secret joy." (5:pg.206)

"Then, on the very hot June 17th of 1937, our Mrs. Lake, who as a rule is a model of decorum, came sweating decorously into my office with a paper cup of iced coffee for me,

set it decorously on my desk, accepted my
thanks, dropped a hankerchief on the floor
as she turned to leave, bent decorously down
to retrieve it, and most undaintily - oh, most
indecorously - broke wind, virtually in my
coffee.
 "'Oh, *excuse* me!' she gasped, and blushed,
and fled. But ah, the fart hung heavy in the
humid air, long past the lady's flight. It
hung, it lalled, it wisped; it miscegenated
with the smoke of my cigar, caressed the bead-
ing oil on the skin of my nose, lay obscenely
on the flat of my desk, among my briefs and
papers. It was everywhere, but I had learned,
even then, to live with nature and my fellow
animals. I didn't flinch; I didn't move.
Through its dense invisible presence I regard-
ed my oracular wall, and this time fruitfully."
(5:pg.103-4)

BASSOON

 We are told that the bassoon is the "farting
instrument" of the orchestra. (30:pg.872) This
becomes evident in Hector Berlioz's *Symphonie
Fantastique* and even more so in Richard
Strauss' *Till Eulenspiegel's Merry Pranks*.
Both symphonic fantasies hang their protagon-
ists at the pieces' climax and true to life,
they both lose control... For musical connois-
seurs only.

BATHTUBS

 It has been related to me that a) there is a
class of people who fart in bathtubs and bite
the bubbles; they are sometimes called "snork-
les" (30:pg.874); and b) something about Polish
bubble baths? (Personal communication) (See
also BEER)

BEANS

Everybody knows what eating beans is suppose
to do, fartologically speaking. The increase
of the fartician's ability occurs about four
hours after the intake of these flatulent pro-
ducers. Yet did you know that some beans work
more efficiently than others? Dr. Louis B.
Rockland of the Western Regional Research Lab-
oratory of the U.S. Dept. of Agriculture in
Berkeley, California has found out the levels
of gas production for ten kinds of beans and
has listed them in decreasing order: #1 produces the most gas, #10 the least. (44)

1. Soybeans
2. Pink Beans
3. Black Beans
4. Pinto Beans
5. California Small White Beans
6. Great Northern Beans
7. Lima Beans (baby)
8. Garbanzos
9. Lima Beans (large)
10. Blackeyes

For those health food advocates who insist
on the use of soybeans it should be stated
that cooking soybeans with an equal amount of
rice eliminates two-thirds of the flatulence
as well as increasing the amount of usable pro-
tein.

Probably more important than any of the above
information is this youthful advertisement for
the virtuosity of the bean:

Beans, beans, the musical fruit
The more you eat, the more you toot
The more you toot, the better you feel
We should have beans at every meal. (41:pg.378)

BECKETT, SAMUEL (1906-   )

See FREQUENCY.

14

BEER

The drinking of beer is traditionally suppose to promote flatulence. (30:pg.874) Unfortunately drunkenness is also promoted and fizzles predominate.

A joke occurs to me:

A man taking a bath in a hotel, farts in the tub. A minute later a bell boy knocks at the door and comes in with a bottle of beer on a tray. "I didn't order any beer," says the man. Bellboy: "But I distinctly heard you say, 'Hey bub, bring up a bottle of Budweiser.'" (30:pg.874)

BELCH

This is an eructation of air or gas *exclusively from the stomach*. (See also AEROPHAGE, BURP, ERUCTATION) (41:pg.165)

BEL-PHEGOR

See CREPITUS.

BIBLIOTHECA SCATOLOGICA

This curious collection of learning has no author claiming it, nor any place or date of publication attached to it. But it does list 133 treatises upon flatulence, some gross, some course, yet one or two quite erudite. Some examples are:

#88: *Eloge du Pet*
#91: "An Essay Upon Wind" by Charles James Fox (celebrated English orator) published anonymously.
#123: *Physiologia crepitus ventris* of Rod. Goclenius, Frankfort and Leopsic, 1607.

BORBORYGMUS (pl. -mi)

"The sounds of borborygmi,
  amongst the lovers' kind,
  So rumbles the pretty poetess,
  borborygmus of the mind."
(attributed to Edward R. Eabos)

Borborygmus is actually the rumbling, squeezing - *burping and farting* - sounds of a noisy abdomen, caused by the movement of gas and juices in the intestines. People usually associate this noise with hunger. (41:pg.165-6 & personal communication)

BOTTLING

See COLORATION.

BOTTOM BURP

See FART.

BOURKE, CAPTAIN JOHN G.

In 1891, Lowdermilk and Co. of Washington (D.C.?) published a book entitled *Scatologic Rites of All Nation - A Disertation upon the employment of excrementitious remedial agents in religion, therapeutics, divination, witchcraft, love-philtres, etc., in all parts of the globe, by CAPTAIN JOHN G. BOURKE, Third Cavalry, U.S.A.* Here is what is listed under "Flatulence" in the index:

"of fairies; flatulence would kill the Eskimo god 'Torngarsuk,' if witchcraft were going on in a house; the Devil put to flight by flatu-

lence; flatulence avoided by the Hebrews while
at prayer, also by the Parsis; considered a
deadly insult by Bedouins and Afghans; a contest for championship among the Arabs; adored
by the Romans, by the Egyptians, by the Hebrews,
by the Moabites, by the Assyrians, in the worship of Bel-Phegor; the bibliography of the
subject; tenures of land in England by flatulence; toll of flatulence exacted of prosti-
tutes who for the first time crossed the bridge
of Montluc in France; called 'Sir Reverence'
by the Irish immigrants to the United States;
in games in England; Satan 'lets a f--t,' in
the old Moralities; the punishment for, among
small boys in Philadelphia, Pa.; in obscene
tales." (9:pg.489)

BREAKING WIND

Breaking wind is the same as farting prig-
gishly, no matter how loud or rancid it may
be. It is safe to assume that if a child "cuts
the cheese," if you're over thirty *he really
"broke wind;"* if under thirty, *he merely farted.* Sometimes known as *passing* wind or *making*
wind. (personal communication)

BREWER'S FART, TO LET A

This phrase is occasionally followed by
"grains and all," thus suggesting its meaning:
to foul oneself. It was used around 1700-1850
at a time when it was believed that when diar-
rhea strikes, "one's arse was not to be trusted with a fart." (35)

BURP

Burping is an eructation of air or gas *exclusively from the esophageal area*. (See also AEROPHAGE, BELCH, ERUCTATION) (41:pg.165-6)

Burp has another meaning which is very interesting for the fartologist, as *burping a baby* to cause the baby to "eructate" by patting or rubbing its back, *"especially to relieve flatulence after feeding."* (38)

CACKLING FART

When a hen farts it is solid and white. It is an egg or "cackling fart." (35:pg.119)

CARMINITIVE

Calamus tea, camomile, lovage, marjoram, oil of peppermint, peppermint tea, valerian tea, cascailla bark and yarrow are all carminitives, that is, agents used to relieve colic, gripping or flatulence, or to expell gas from the intestines.

CHAUCER, GEOFFREY (1340?-1400)

During the life and times of Geoffrey Chaucer it was not unusual to find numerous jests and stories centered around a fart. Therefore it is not surprising to find Chaucer becoming infect-

ed with the fartological realms and perpetrating a jest or two of his own.

For example, in amongst his *Canterbury Tales*
we find the "Miller's Tale" telling us how
when Absolon kisses Alison's "ers" by mistake,
he thinks of her face and is at first bewilder-
ed by its hair. The second time, expecting the
same prank, he seeks for her arse by asking,
"Spek, sweete byrd, I noot nat where thou art,"
whereupon Nicholas "anon leet fle a fart, As
gret as it had been a thonder dint," and meets
his disaster.

CLEMENS, SAMUEL

See TWAIN, MARK.

COLORATION

Coloration and bottling of farts is in its
very early stages. Information is hard to come
by, yet if one is truly interested, what little
is known can be obtained at the Fart Formula
Factory. I will, though, allow one interesting
story to slip by. It has come to my attention
that quite recently a famous New York City artist (whose name I will not mention) surreptitiously procured a small vial containing
"posterior flatus" from the late Marilyn Monroe.
I understand an extremely high price was paid
for this precious jewel. (21)

COPROPHILIA

Coprophilia is a psychiatric term given to a
person who has an extreme interest in feces.
It is logical to assume that such a person would
be equally interested in the flatulating processes. In fact, it is not an uncommon accusa-
tion against fartology and fartologists alike,
especially if one proclaims to be an authority

on farts and farting and has the audacity to
actually write a book upon this subject, that
the logic be reversed and thus any given fartologist must therefore be a coprophiliac too.
Let me proclaim here and get it out once and
for all! I am not and have never been a coprophiliac; I am not and have never been a flatophile (see FLATOPHILE); and furthermore, I am
not and have never been a *Christian!* (See OLD
FART) (38:pg.323)

COUNT OF TRUMPET

The Count of Trumpet authored a book entitled
L'Art de Peter (The Art of Farting) which was
published with the rubric "En Westphalie," in
"the Year of Liberty, 1776." The book is sup-
posedly "witty." It is the result of P.T.N.
Hurtoult's anonymous translation of *Sclopetar-
ius and Goclenius* (in Dornan's *Amphitheatrum*,
1619). (15&30:pg.858)

CREPITATION

To crepitate is to make a "crackling sound."
Seeing as a fart can loosely be heard as a
"crackling sound," the term has become syn-
onymous with the word "fart." (See FART) (41)

CREPITATION CONTEST

"Your narrator - Sydney F. Brown" is the name
of a Canadian sports-announcer whose voice is
mimicked to call the shots in a Crepitation
Contest. It was recorded in Toronto, 1943, and
privately issued in both the United States and
Canada on three 78 rpm records. More recently
it has been reissued on a single long-playing
33 rpm record with the abbreviated title, *"The
Contest."* The recording is a "burlesque account, told in a breathless radio-announcer

style, of the prize competition between the
English champion and the Australian contender,
who wins with a particularly rich and vibrating
'flutterblast,' and the final catastrophe. This
is one kind of folklore that cannot be reproduced, even onomatopoetically in print." (30:
pg.873)

Salvador Dali tells about a record he once
heard upon which a Club of American Windbreak-
ers performed. His aesthetic endorsement of it
was succinctly described in a single word:
"precious." Unfortunately, he neglected to say
anymore. (15:pg.53)

CREPITUS

Crepitus was one of the many Roman gods. In
Latin his name means "a crackling sound" and
is intended to refer to flatulence. The ancient
Romans thus worshiped the Fart, animating it
into a god. "I assert that they used *to adore*
... stinking and filthy privies and water-clos-
ets; and, what is viler and yet more abominable,
what is an occasion for our tears and not to
be borne with so much as mentioned by name,
they adored the noise and wind of the stomach
when it expels from itself any cold or flatulence; and other things of the same which ...
it would be a shame to name or describe," so
tells us Torquemada.

Capt. John G. Bourke traced the god Crepitus
to Egyptian roots relating him to Bel-Phegor.
"Le Pet (fart)," he tells us, "was an ancient
Egyptian goddess; she was the personification
of a natural function."

In the second century AD Minucius Felix wrote
that "Crepitus ... was perhaps only a carica-
ture conceived by the jesters of that time.
Menage however affirms that the Pelusians (a
people of lower Egypt) worshiped *le Pet.*"

And much later Charles Percy, MD wrote in *A
View of the Levant* (1743) that "the ancient
Pelusians ... did (amongst other whimsical,

chimerical objects of veneration and worship)
venerate a Fart, which they worshiped under
the symbol of a swelled paunch." (9:chapter 21
& 41:chapter 10)

CUT

   A finger; a leg; one; one's finger; the
cheese. (See FART)

DALI, SALVADOR (1904-)

Salvador Dali, perhaps not surprisingly, was the man who first made me aware of the need for an exclusive and definitive study within the realm of the fartological concern. Somewhere amongst his writings he tells us how Freud opened up the area of sexuality to free discussion but that scatology, though extant, was still taboo. Indeed, he had his own style of transmitting that message, but as already stated, the source is forgotten, so my own version will have to do.

There are many other fartistic statements that have been penned by Dali, and at one time they found a place in the present work. In fact it was then written that these statements *"should be included in any book upon fartology"* (italics added presently). But you will not find them here because I felt that the expense and extravagant terms associated with the permission to quote them was out of my budget. I'm sorry, but the cost was too high considering that it extended to only a small number of printed books... Georges Borchart, Incorporated - do you read me?

I can tell you where to look though. Go to your public library and ask for Salvador Dali's *Diary of a Genius* (15a) and look at pages 34-5 and 59-60. You will be well rewarded.

My own retaliation was to peruse Dali's other books hoping to find a book whose copyright was controlled elsewhere. This is what I found.

"I hardly fart at all anymore, and only on awakening, very melodiously. This morning, I dedicated my fart to St. Augustine, prince of petomanes, for I am in a mystical phase." (15b: pg.268)

DANTE (1265-1321)

Throughout all of Dante's writing, I find it almost unbelievable that he only mentions farting once. Canto xxi, lines 136-139 of Dante's *Inferno* tells us that:

"Devils stick their tongues out at their leader as a form of salute, to which their leader responds with a fart."

DAVIES, JOHN (1569-1626)

Sir John Davies, an English poet and lawyer living in Middleborough placed this short epigram "In Leucam" in his *Epigrammes and Elergies by J.D. and C.M.* (28:pg.27)

"Leuca in presence once a fart did lett,
 Some laught a little, she forsooke the place,
 And mad with shame, did eke her glove forget,
 Which she returned to fetch with bashfull grace:
    And when she would have said, this is my glove,
    My fart (quoth she) which did more laughter move."

DE VERE, EDWARD (1550-1604)

Edward DeVere was the 17th Earl of Oxford. John Aubrey tells us that, "this Earl of Oxford, making his low obeisance to Queen Elizabeth, happened to let a Fart, at which he was so a- bashed and ashamed that he went to Travell, seven years. On his returne the Queen welcomed him home, and sayd, My lord, I had forgott the Fart." (4)

DEVILS

In the dealings of fartology, it is not un- common to come face to face with the undoubted creators of the fart: devils and demons. Here is an example:

"A milker, believing that at the moment of death his soul escapes through the anus, ar- ranged that his wife and the priest pull him to the ends of the bed so as to witness the event. The phenomenon of rectal flatulence is now ob- served, when suddenly, to the consternation of the wife and the priest, a demon appears and placing a sack over the dying man's anus, catches the rectal gas and flies off in sul- phurous vapor." (9) (See also DANTE)

DOGS

The poor dog. It is the dog that always gets the blame. From John Selden's *Table Talk* (ante 1654; ed. 1869, pg. 27):

"The Bishops being put out of the House, whom will they lay the fault upon now? When the Dog is beat out of the Room, where will they lay the stink?" (30:pg.859)

DON JUAN, Yaqui Sorcerer

Don Juan, that mysterious Mexican Indian sorcerer that has become so famous through the books of Carlos Castaneda, once declared:

"I'm sorry, but Carlos Castaneda does not allow *anyone* to quote from his books."

No, Don Juan did not really say *that!* But what he did say can be found on page 164 of the paperback edition of *A Separate Reality.* (12)

DRY AS A POPCORN FART

If you are really, really thirsty and in dire need of a bit of liquid refreshment, as a consequence, your oral cavity is no doubt "as dry as a popcorn fart." This implies that popcorn farts are probably opposite in quality to fizzles or brewer's farts. A bit of experimentation should be done in this area for clarification. (Personal communication)

EABOS, EDWARD R. (1854-1945)

As painters can detect hundreds and hundreds of variations of colors, and musicians can differentiate between many, many sounds; Prof. Eabos began to build his sense of smell. He came into the world of smell at a very early age. Not until later did he find that his life's work as an artist was to make him an outcaste in all areas of society; sneered at by all those who would not and could not accept an Artist of Smell. Few people have ever and will ever enjoy and realize the true genius of his life's work of putting together different smells to produce new ones unknown to any man alive. He told us once that the only person that understood was Erik Satie (the early contemporary composer) who took what inspiration he could to write his *"Trois Gnossienne."* But upon introducing Prof. Eabos to Debussy, Prof. Eabos was once again an outcaste, now even of the art world. True fart smells was only a small portion of his "smell cosmology" but his work was extremely important in opening a new area of Fartology. (36)

EDISON, THOMAS (1847-1931)

An early and individual explorer of fartology was America's Thomas A. Edison. He was greatly intriqued by the motor force that can be accumulated in our lower areas. He explored and experimented with the possibilities of aviation for light weight men and young boys. For his experiment he used a young man in his family's employ. Inducing him to swallow a large quantity of Seidlitz powders, a great amount of gases were generated.

Records show that he blamed the boy rather than the motive power involved for the failure of the experiment. No further studies of this sort have been attempted since. (26)

EMPEROR CLAUDIUS (10bc-54ad)

In Michel de Montaigne's *Autobiography* it is told that some Emperor of the past decreed that anyone may "let fly as we will," anywhere. Well, actually, Emperor Claudius only *contemplated* such a decree as this. What led Claudius to such contemplations was the death of one of his subject whose death was caused by gastric disturbances. The facts about Emperor Claudius were reported by Roman biographer and anti-quarian Suetonius. (See MONTAIGNE) (32)

Regardless of *any* politician's law, I'd like to pass on this bit of advise: (Learmont, *Poeme* 1791; Scott, Antiquary, 1816 EDD.)

"To piss and fart,
Is good for the heart."

ERUCTATION

Eructation, the act upon which lies *all of the eructologist's concerns*, is the *ejection of wind or gas* spasmodically from anywhere within the body, yet *exclusively out through the mouth*. This includes both *belching* (from whence the air or gas is from the stomach) and *burping* (esophageal). Being the absolute opposite of flatulation it becomes immediately important for the practicing fartologist. (34&41) (See also BELCH, BURP)

EUPHEMISMS

As with most things considered obscene, farts are a part of our daily human life. As much as the *civilized* sector of mankind would like to abolish their existences the rest of us, yearning to keep in touch with our humanity, have created an underground language so to be able to talk about "it" anytime and anyplace without the fear of Big Brother Morality digging his or her claws into our flesh to press the button of guilt. Furthermore, seeing as farts and farting along with the other "soft" and "hard" obscenities are essential to be talked and taught about, more often than not *each family* in the Western World has created its own "outlaw language" for the continuance of this secret learning within each family. Clearly, one can see that a definitive listing of all the fart's euphemisms is nearly impossible. Yet there does exist a secondary system of euphemisms that are used as a means of discussing this subject among various families. These families are clearly taking a chance, but aren't the rewards well worth it?

Here is a short sampling from the *secondary system of euphemisms:*

1. Bottom burp
2. Breaking wind

3. Crepitate
 4. Cut a finger (ca. 1909)
 5. Cut a leg (ca. 1909)
 6. Cut one
 7. Cut one's finger (ca. 1909)
 8. Cut the cheese
 9. Fartkin
10. Fartnic
11. Flatulate
12. Flatus
13. Gas
14. Lay one
15. Lay a stinker
16. Let fly
17. Let loose
18. Making wind
19. Passing wind
20. Posterior flatus
21. Wind

FART

A fart is a fart is a fart is an anal escape
of wind. Audible or silent, odoriferous or
scentless, as a verb or as a noun, rancid or
the fragrant smell of lilacs in springtime: a
fart is a fart is a fart. From the Old English
foertan, which has the same meaning, also signifying *to explode*, it became "soft" obscenity
(that is, taboo) around 1750 when it also came
to be used as a term of contempt for a worth-
less person - or even someone you didn't quite
like. It has also come to mean *not to care* as
in "I don't give a fart for..." or "it's not
worth a fart." (31&35&46)

FART ABOUT (*or "around"*)

Wasting time, playing around or just plain
dawdling are all ways to "fart about." (35)

FARTANDO, DON

Don Fartando, also known as Don Fart in Hando (35), is the pseudonym for the Spanish author of *The Benefit of Farting Explained*. It was "wrote in Spanish by a Prof. of Bumbast in the University of Craccow." The fourth edition was revised by a "College of Fizz-icians." (15) It was translated into English by Obadiah Fizle. (35) Eric Partridge saw a 10th edition listed in a 1933 bookseller's catalogue. Perhaps someday this work will find a place in the present anthology.

FART-ARSED MECHANIC

If you happened to be walking down a London street in the year 1925 and you also happened to be dropping things and occasionally stumbling or tripping, someone would have undoubtedly noticed that you were a very "fart-arsed mechanic" or clumsy person. (35)

FARTARSING ABOUT (or "around")

During World War II when for a lark a soldier hopped into a motored vehicle and began driving about with no exact destination in mind, he was merely "fartarsing around." (35)

FART-CATCHER

This catchy phrase was a slang term for a footman or a valet (he walks behind). It was used when footmen and valets were popular, 1750-1900. (35)

Seeing such a phrase fall by the wayside seemed such a pity that around 1930 it was revised to the angry protests of homosexuals everywhere upon whose description it was placed. (35)

FART-DANIEL

A "fart-daniel" is, in an attempt towards morality, usually defined as *"the pudendum muliebre"* or *"woman's pudendum,"* both being obscure euphemisms for the woman's vagina. It's semantic derivation is obscure yet a (hilariously?) confusing attempt was made by Eric Partridge in his *Dictionary of Slang.*

"I surmise that fart=farth, alleged to = a litter of pigs, and that *daniel* - (Cf. Antony pig) - is the youngest pig (see E.D.D. at *daniel & farth)*, hence that this strange term is orig. dial. (not in E.D.D.); it may, however, be merely a misprint for "fare-daniel", dial. for a sucking pig that is the youngest of a litter." (35)

And how one gets from pigs to vaginas, I'll never know.

The vagina is instead sometimes called a *"farting-clapper"* by workmen. (35)

FARTER

See PETOMANIAC.

FARTING-CRACKERS

In the language of the underworld of the late 17th and 18th centuries, "farting-crackers" were identical to breeches. (35)

FART-FACE

"Fart-face" is used exclusively as an insult. A variation is *"fart-head."* (46)

FARTICIAN

Any person who is interested and/or studies farts and farting. Also known as a *fartologist* or *fartist*. (37)

FARTICK

Diminutive of fart. (See FART) (35)

FART IN A BOTTLE, LIKE A

If you are flustered, agitated and jumpy; if you find yourself running around in small circles; your friends and relatives would surely liken you to a "fart in a bottle" for you'd be "rushing around not knowing which hole to come out." Also described as "like a fart in a colander," it is believed to have been around since mid-19th century. (35)

FART IN A GALE, LIKE A

Being in Western Canada without any money and absolutely nowhere to go, you would be "like a fart in a gale;" that is, utterly helpless.

A "fart in a gale*wind*" however describes a meaningless speech made by a politician, teacher, or other in authority. (35&46)

FART IN A WIND STORM, AS MUCH CHANCE AS A

In Canada having "as much chance as a fart in a wind storm" is as good as having no chance at all, whereas in England one can *become* a "fart in a wind storm" if one happened to be puny and ineffective. (35)

FARTING FANNY

The shell of a heavy German gun operated in the Arras sector during World War I. It was the jargon of artillery men and is now considered historical. "The War was trundling on quite peacefully as they walked and jogged eastwards towards it, with the occasional clang of Farting Fanny's arrival in caverous Arras." -*Blaker* (35)

FARTING SHOT

You've just had an amazing quarrel - there's no way to win and you are sick of it. Still angry you leave the room and just as you exit you "let loose a rouzer." (Farting shot = parting shot.)

I've also heard of this vulgar comment used upon exiting an elevator where the "butt" of the joke is left entrapped.

The term "farting shot" originated around 1940. (35)

FARTING-TRAP

In the early days of automobiles, the English and the Irish would often be seen on sunny summer days out for a leisurely ride in their "farting-traps" or cars. The term is now obsolete. (35)

FARTKIN

Diminutive of fart. (See FART) (35)

FARTLEBERRIES

"Fartleberries" was once a rather colorful

36

way of describing any excrement that happened
to cling to the anal hair. It has not been in
use since 1900. (35)

FART LOVER

   To call someone a "fart lover" is most likely
intended to insult by implying that one is a
flatophile or petomaniac. In some cases where
no insult is intended it can be used as a state-
ment of fact: one who indeed has affection for
flatulence. (46)

FARTOLOGY

   A SCIENTIFIC INQUIRY INTO THE NATURE OF FARTS
AND FARTING AND THE EXPLORATION INTO THE DEVEL-
OPMENT OF BETTER FARTS IN DEDICATION TO THE
HIGHEST FOR ARTISTIC AND RELIGIOUS ENDEAVORS:
Instructions for recording quantitative anal-
ysis and observational data.

(1) Keep a record of food eaten and the time and
    day when devoured.

(2) Always record the time and day when each
    fart is discharged.

(3) Specify the physical attributes connected
    with each disturbance:

    W. duration = a) too quick b) noticeable
       c) healthy d) long e) amazed

    X. amplitude = a) silent b) barely audible
       c) healthy d) loud e) amazed

    Y. $smell^1$ = a) none b) faintly c) smelled
       d) smelly e) had to leave the room (or
       highly acute perversion)

    Z. $smell^2$ = description ie. dog dung, hard
       boiled eggs, pansies, etc. Try to be
       accurate and always strive for new and
       exciting nasal environments.

(4) Try to state conditions, emotions, sensations, etc. if eroticism or perversion becomes connected with out-blow.

(5) If a bowel movement is associated with e-mission state condition of turd (or turd particles).

Obtain a notebook and immediately begin to keep clear and articulate data of your daily intake and output. Strive for imaginative and beautiful results. Comments are always welcome as is individuality. Offspring experiments such as ignitional effects, coloration and bottling are interesting areas open for individual investigations. All information dealing with the subject of farts is welcomed. I assure you, you will be rewarded not only intellectually but also spiritually and emotionally. (37)

> *The answer my friend,*
> *Is blowing in the wind.*
> —Bob Dylan

FART-SUCKER

The term "fart-sucker" is now obsolete - but not yet the fart-sucker, for a fart-sucker is identical to a human parasite. Then again, I would not doubt the term's occasional accuracy when considered literally. What a dreadful species *you* are. (35)

FEE, FIE, FOE, FUM

The Apache Indians of Western North America have a myth analogous to the story of *Jack and the Beanstalk*, yet the Apache's giant was inclined to follow a somewhat stronger scent. Hence, the rationale for the title of the present work. (9&41)

FIZLE, OBADIAH

See FARTANDO, DON.

FIZZLE

"Fizzles" may be low pitched or even silent. They are characterized by dampness, strong odor, and often visible stains. They can often develope into a "brewer's fart." Thus a fizzle well emphasizes that "a fart is the cry of an imprisoned turd," a phrase that was poetically derived in the 1930's. Fizzle has been around a long, long time. (30&35)

FLATOPHILE

"Flatophile" is the psychological term given to the literal "fart-lover." Let us quote from the case history of a *chronic flatophile* found in the writings of Sandor Ferenczi.

"A young homosexual who without much ado made use of even the vulgar designations for the sexual parts and their functions, refused for two hours long to utter aloud the commoner expression for the word "flatus" which had occurred to him. He sought to avoid it by all possible circumlocutions, foreign words, euphemisms, etc. After the resistance against the word was overcome, however, he was able to penetrate much deeper into the previously barren analysis of his anal-erotism. (18:pg.114)

"The young homosexual who had displayed such strong opposition to uttering the obscene word for "flatus" developed in infancy an extraordinary love of odour and coprophilia, and his over lenient father did not prevent him from indulging these inclinations even on his own body (the father's). The association, inseparable from this time forward of the idea of unusually strong repression of the pleasure

39

of dirt and smell; hence also the great un-
pleasantness in mentioning such matters. That
it was the obscene term for intestinal gas which
was so much more intolerable to him than any
circumlocution had its reason in childhood,...
the intimate connection between obscenity and
the parental complex was thus the strongest re-
pressing force.

"The infantile interest for the sound accompanying the emission of intestinal gas was not
without influence on his choice of profession.
He became a musician." (18:pg.121)

Farting and homosexuality are often related.
Consider the following joke as an example.

"Nancy boy in shoe shop up on ladder, reaching
for a boot-box farts. Other nancy boy at foot
of step sighs: 'Why speak of love when there's
work to be done?'" (30:pg.877)

FLATULENCE

The accumulation of gas in the stomach and
lower intestines and the resulting escapes of
the gas therewith. Sounds like farting to me!

FLATUS

Usually considered as a synonym to the noun
fart, "flatus" is actually everything a fart
is - except the sound. As a Latin word for
gas or air, it implies neither location nor
direction, but everyone knows better. (41:pg.
165)

FRANKLIN, BEN (1706-1790)

Ben Franklin had a vast amount of interests.
Many know him as statesman, writer, inventor,
scientist, etc., but very few are aware of his

contributions in the area of fartology. His
major concern was to relieve the anxiety and
embarrassment that often accompany the farter
by attempting to chemically relieve the odor
from flatulence.
His most famous essay written on this subject
was first presented before the Royal Academy of
Brussels. It is reproduced here in full.

"I have perused your late mathematical prize
question, proposed in lieu of one in natural
philosophy for the ensuing year... I conclude
therefore that you have given this question instead of a philosophical, or as the learned ex-
press it, a *physical* one, because you could not
at this time think of a physical one that promised greater *utility*... Permit me then humbly
to propose one of that sort for your consider-
ation, and through you, if you approve it, for
the serious inquiry of learned physicians,
chemists, etc., of this enlightened age.

"It is universally well known, That in di-
gesting our common Food, there is created or
produced in the Bowels of human Creatures, a
great Quantity of Wind.

"That the permitting this Air to escape and
mix with the Atmosphere, is usually offensive
to the Company, from the fetid Smell that accompanies it.

"That all well-bred People therefore, to a-
void giving such Offence, forcibly restrain the
Efforts of Nature to discharge that Wind.

"That so retain'd contrary to Nature, it not
only gives frequenty great present Pain, but
occasions future Diseases, such as habitual
Cholics, Ruptures, Tympanies, &c. often des-
tructive of the Constitution, & sometimes of
Life itself.

"Were it not for the odiously offensive Smell
accompanying such Escapes, polite people would
probably be under no more Restraint in discharging such Wind in Company, than they are in
spitting, or in blowing their Noses.

"My Prize Question therefore should be, To

discover some Drug wholesome & not disagreeable,
to be mix'd with our common Food, or Sauces,
that shall render the Natural Discharges, of
Wind from our Bodies, not only inoffensive, but
agreeable as Perfumes.

"That this is not a chimerical Project, and
altogether impossible, may appear from these
Considerations. That we already have some Knowledge of Means capable of Varying that Smell.
He that dines on stale Flesh, especially with
much Addition of Onion, shall be able to afford
a Stink that no Company can tolerate; while he
that has lived for some Time on Vegetables only,
shall have that Breath so pure as to be insen-
sible to the most delicate Noses; and if he can
manage so as to avoid the Report, he may any
where give Vent to his Griefs, unnoticed. But
as there are many to whom an entire Vegetable
Diet would be inconvenient, and as a little
Quick-Lime thrown into a Fakes will correct the
amazing Quantity of fetid Air arising from the
vast Mass of putrid Matter contain'd in such
Places, and render it rather pleasing to the
Smell, who knows but that a little Powder of
Lime (or some other thing Equivalent) taken in
our Food, or perhaps a Glass of Limewater drank
at Dinner, may have the same Effect on the Air
produc'd in and issuing from our Bowels? This
is worth the Experiment. Certain it is also that
we have the Power of changing by slight Means
the Smell of another Discharge, that of our
Water. A few stems of Asparagus eaten, shall
give our Urine a disagreeable Odour; and a Pill
of Turpentine no bigger than a Pea, shall bestow on it the pleasing Smell of Violets. And
why should it be thought more impossible in
Nature, to find Means of making a Perfume of
our Wind than of our Water?

"For the Encouragement of this Enquiry, (from
the immortal Honour to be reasonably expected
by the inventor) let it be considered of how
small Importance to Mankind, or to how small a
Part of Mankind have been useful those Discov-
eries in Science that have heretofore made Phil-

osophers famous. Are there twenty Men in
Europe at this Day, the happier, or even the
easier for any Knowledge they have pick'd out
of Aristotle? What Comfort can the Vortices of
Descartes give to a Man who has Whirlwinds in
his Bowels! The Knowledge of Newton's mutual
Attraction of the Particles of Matter, can if
afford Ease to him who is rack'd by their mutual Repulsion, and the cruel Distensions it
occasions? The Pleasure arising to a few Philosophers, from seeing, a few Times in their
Life, the Threads of Light untwisted, and separated by the Newtonian Prism into seven Colours,
can it be compared with the Ease and Comfort
every Man living might feel seven times a Day,
by discharging freely the Wind from his Bowels?
Especially if it be converted into a Perfume:
For the Pleasures of one Sense being little in-
ferior to those of another, instead of pleasing
the Sight he might delight the Smell of those
about him, & make Numbers happy, which to a
benevolent Mind must afford infinite Satisfac-
tion. The generous Soul, who now endeavours to
find out whether the Friends he entertains like
best Claret or Burgundy, Champagne or Madeira,
would then inquire also whether they chose Musk
or Lilly, Rose or Bergamot, and provide accord-
ingly. And surely such a Liberty of Ex-pressing
one's Scentiment, and pleasing one another, is
of infinitely more Importance to human Happi-
ness than that Liberty of the Press, or of a-
busing one another, which the English are so
ready to fight   and die for.
   "In short, this Invention, if completed,
would be, as Bacon expresses it, bringing Philosophy home to Men's Business and Bosoms. And
I cannot but conclude, that in comparison therewith, for universal and continual UTILITY, the
Science of the Philosophers abovementioned,
even with the Addition, Gentlemen, of your
Figure quelconque" and the Figures inscrib'd
in it, are all together, scarcely worth a
FART-HING."

Ben Franklin wrote this sometime in 1780. After his death it lay quietly inside the Library of Congress for 150 years at which time it was finally published and made somewhat accessible to the public. I was first made aware of it when I saw the piece advertised in the back of some forgotten magizine. Printed in an illegible tiny script typing style upon crispy paper made to look old, it cost me a mere $5. Do you think it was worth it?

FREQUENCY

Alas, the account of the man who farts .267 times every minute cannot tell his story here. (See instead 6) Grove Press, a storehouse of "scurrilous" material itself, passed moral judgement against my work and disallowed permission to quote from any books whose copyright is still held by the aforementioned house. Funny, but it was that publisher that had the greatest number of books with fart quotes contained within!

Well, I had gotten a nice little letter back from Grove Press that briefly stated, "permission not granted." There contained one "I am sorry" but not a single reason why not. To find this out, I called them up and the woman in charge of permissions spluttered out the existence of a *moral charge against me*. Not by her, mind you, *but by someone higher up!*

In any case, infuriated I "ripped off" the letter that follows to defend my cause. Obviously, it didn't work. I don't think they like me over there at Grove Press, *and after reading this they're going to like me a hell of a lot less!*

Dear Grove Press,

This letter concerns the fact that my request for permission to quote from Samuel Beckett's *Molloy* and from *My Secret Life* was denied. Let me state my case.

My *Dictionary of Fartology* (more properly
called *Fee, Fie, Foe, Fum* due to an Apache Indian myth curiously similar to the Jack and the
Beanstalk tale except for the scent followed)
can be described with a single word: "erudite."
It finds merit in the following ways: It is
folklore that exists and is denied. It becomes
humorous in that it is possible to bring together so much material to a subject in which
it is believed there is none. It attempts sur-
realism in perpetrating a myth about a "science
of fartology" in the tradition and style of
Norman Douglas' limerick commentaries or as I
prefer - through a conglomerate of fact and
fancy akin to Borges. It *does not* promulgate
"immorality" (that is the kind of immorality
fought against by Gershon Legman or Wilhelm
Reich).

Where it delves into infantilism, it does so
to come to terms with Freud; where it delves
into sado-masochism (and it is subtle), it does
so to come to terms with Christianity: of which
I am neither affiliated.

It's subtle premise (except where made expli-
cit in the forward) is to proselytize the reader into the act of *thinking* - about anything -
and a plea for freedom of thought, even if that
of a paranoid construction. From there it presents such a paranoidal structure: the "scurrilous" concept of a new science - (excuse me),
FARTOLOGY. Thus it is a novel based on facts.
And for the serious scholar, each and every
fact is given its precise source.

As far as Mr. Beckett's inclusion - I origin-
ally had him there if only because he thought
and wrote about an aspect of the subject not
mentioned elsewhere: Frequency. Indeed, to quote
him is to jest with him but he is not alone. In
fact there is quite a tradition (especially in
England) behind him (no pun intended). Thus I
also quote from Ben Jonson, Chaucer, John Davies,
Swift, Robert Herrick, George Gascoigne, John
Heywood and Thomas More; the Arabian Nights,

Aristophanes and Rabelais; Ben Franklin, Mark Twain and Ogden Nash; John Barth, Thomas Berger, Tom Robbins, Leslie Fiedler and the astronomer/celebrity Carl Sagan. And this is just a sampling. Not bad company.

Further, the chosen quote itself can be considered Beckett in a nutshell, if you will. He comes upon something (anything, even f--ting) and attaches to it a great profundity thus giving some substance and meaning to his life only to analyze it away. In a matter of seconds he is again left empty. Or don't you agree?

On now to *My Secret Life*. What a book, and what a guy! That curious document is far from a healthy rendition of the human soul. But it exists, eh? And it more than thoroughly discusses a hidden aspect of Victorian life (and perhaps *not* so Victorian). It is an area of denied existence, not unlike some aspects of my own subject... And Grove Press brought it to the surface for human inspection.

My purpose in writing a book about ... and my plans to self-publish and market it are two different things. I have other projects and need money to persue them. And I believe that people will buy such a book. (I like to imagine such people buying the book in hopes of satisfying some "dirty" aspect of their psyches - and then getting some education in the process.) But in the final analysis, I'm printing the book in hopes of making some money.

In conclusion, I hope that this letter will help you to re-evaluate your position on the matter of granting me permission to quote from the aforementioned books.

Sincerely yours,

E. Slove Prombles

E. Slove Prombles

(This letter is reprinted from *Fizzles Galore: The Letters of Fartology.*)

GAMES

Many young children (and some adults) make a game out of farting. For example, when I was young, if a friend happened to notice a tell-tale odor permeating the area around us, and then if that person were to say anything about it, the rest of us would chant, "Whoever smelt it, dealt it!" Once this was exclaimed, the real culprit was let off the hook.

Another way of getting off the hook was to engage in a game I'll call "thumbs up." In this game whoever happens to fart (or is the first to notice another person's fart) immediately puts his thumb to his forehead, the rest of his fingers forming a fist pointing upwards. All that spot this action taking place must immediately follow suit. It is the last person to get their thumb to their forehead who gets pinned as the fart's creator. Usually, the true creator will be the first one to get their thumb in place, but by admitting to the deed in such a manner, the farter is absolved from all guilt.

A similar game is called "slugs." A person who happens to fart will immediately confess to the fact by yelling out the words, "No slugs!" Thus exclaimed, all guilt is absolved. But if he is not quick enough to call this out and is found out, then all the others present are allowed to slug or punch the farter in the arm as punishment.

Surprisingly, both games mentioned have the added effect of causing the participants to *want* to produce as many farts as they possibly can, the louder the better. In fact, what often developes is a contest among the participants and the champ becoming quite proud of his talent will usually be the one to initiate future contests. It is rather like having the winner of a card game becoming the dealer. (personal observations)

GAS

A primitive word referring to the posterior flatus. (See FART)

Another definition for this vulgar word is the fluid that allows one's car to run. When this fluid began to become expensive, America's never ending supply of satirical poets began to think up all kinds of little ditties that they could sell to the media for a lotta money so that there would continue to exist a small elitist group still able to afford to pay the ever rising price of gas. Thus was created the bumper sticker that reads:.

"America needs more gas - eat beans!" (personal observation)

GASCOIGNE, GEORGE (1530-1577)

In George Gascoigne's *The Droome of Doomes*

Day (1576) his description of gluttony has a
prominent place amongst our fartological concerns. Thus we quote a short passage from the
pages of this early fartician.

"Gluttony dothe rayse a great trybute, but
it rendreth a most vyle revenewe. For the more
delicate that the meats bee, so much the more
styncking are the excrements, and ordure made
thereof. He shal doo the more beastly in all
things, which doth most greedely loade and
powre in. He shal break unsavory and loathsome
wynd, both upwardes and downwardes, and make
an abhominable smell and noyse therewith." (22)

And here we record Gascoigne's highly opin-
ionated view of man:

"O vile unworthinesse of mans estate and con-
dicion, & O unworthy estate of mans vilenesse.
Search the trees & the herbes of the Earth,
they bringe forth boughes, leaves, flowers, &
fruits. A man bringeth forth nitts, lyse &
worms. They distill & power out, Oyle, Wyne,
and Balmes, & a man maketh excrements of spet-
tle, pisse, and ordure. They smell & breathe
all sweetenesse of smell & pleasuantnesse,
whereas man belcheth, breaketh wynde and
stincketh..." (22)

GOODFELLOW, ROBIN

Robin Goodfellow is a jolly little elf that
likes to dance and sing. Here is his song!

"When lads and lasses merry be,
 With possets and with juncates fine,
 Unseene of all the company,
 I eat their cakes and sip their wine;
 And to make sport,
 I fart and snort,
 And out the candles I do blow." (10)

GORP

The "guys" from Philadelphia, Pennsylvania
have long learned their lessons bestowed upon
them at the turn of the century (see the latter part of BOURKE). Consequently, an unconventional slang developed in the area and from
among these words *"gorp"* has finally come to
the surface. The onomatopoetic "gorp" is syn-
onymous with an underwater fart. (ca. 1970)
(personal communication)

GUILPIN, EVERARD

An excerpt from Everard Guilpin's *Skialeth-
eia:*

"(Good Lord) that men should have such kennel
                    wits
To thinke so well of a scald railing vaine,
Which soone is vented in beslavered writs.
As when the cholicke in the gutts doth straine,
  With civill conflicts in the same embrac't,
  But let a fart, and then the worst is past."
  (28:pg.48)

HERRICK, ROBERT (1591-1674)

Robert Herrick, the English poet "in whom
the spirit of the ancient classical lyric was
born again," tells us about a man who he apparently had a disliking for. Thus he related
to us the fact that Mr.
"Skoles stinks so deadly, that his Breeches loath
 His dampish Buttocks furthermore to cloath:
 Cloy'd they are up with Arse; but hope, one blast
 Will whirle about, and blow them thence at last."
 (28:pg.61)

HEYWOOD, JOHN (1497-after 1575)

Elizabethan dramatist John Heywood is the
author of a short couplet in which is pointed
out the benefits of farting.

"What winde can there blow, that doth not some
        man please?
 A fart in the blowyng doth the blower ease."
 (28:pg.27)

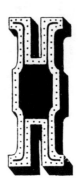

IGNITIONAL EFFECTS

It is indeed true, and people have been putting matches where they'd often wished they
hadn't for years and years. Occasionally path-
ological fermentation occurs in the stomach
and/or lower intestines generating the gas
methane in quantities "sufficient to give rise
to an explosion if the patient *eructates* while
lighting a cigarette." (!) Fortunately this is
rare. But the microbic effect in the lower
intestines instead *always* generates the highly
inflammable and explosive gases hydrogen sul-
fide and hydrogen itself. And it is these
gases that are the cause of so many young men
to "burn their britches behind them." (41:pg.
166)

IMITATION FARTS

There are many ways to imitate a fart but

first, I insist on reminding you of one of your most embarrassing moments. Remember seating yourself in that certain chair at the theater, or at school (or anywhere!) and the friction that caused a rubbing noise that sounded *so much like it* and you were so convinced that everyone was sure you *really did do it* and so you tried to recreate the sound so everyone would know its *real source* and you never could get it to sound quite the same way, could you? Or was it your shoes that rubbed just the wrong way? Anyway, a joke comes to mind:

The First Sound
   A certain man let out a fart in front of a visitor to whom he was talking. He felt so ashamed he wanted to camouflage it, so, as if continuing the sound, he rubbed the chair with his finger, but the visitor said, "Somehow or other, the first sound was most like." (7:pg. 137)

We have all learned as children various ways of creating farting sounds and they were usually used as a means for causing embarrassment in others. The easiest method was to put your tongue between your two lips and to blow out. Another was to cup one hand under the underarm and to flap that arm like a wing. Finally, you may have learned the more difficult art of placing two cupped hands together and creatively pushing and pulling the air in and out of the cavity created between them. This last method I have seen employed on TV by which the imitation farter is able to play simple (and sometimes not so simple) tunes. It appears to make quite a hit with the viewing public. (personal observations)

JOKES

Indeed, there exist a great many jokes about
the flatulent processes and although fartologist G. Legman has claimed, "None of these
jokes seem very funny to ordinary people,"
they do give insight into the psychology of
farting. (See LEGMAN) Perhaps a greater truth
is embodied in this short poem from the Orient:

> Farting-
>   There's nothing funny about it
> When you're living alone.
>
> > *-EMPEKI (17:pg.*
> > *261)*

Most people fraternize and so the jokes do
exist and for some reason continue to be told.
Consequently, here is a small sampling. Further examples can be found by consulting #7,
16, 17, 29 and 30 of the bibliography. (See
also LIMERICKS)

A young lady was eating lunch alone at a

restaurant and couldn't help overhearing a discussion among the four men at a neighboring table.

Said the first man, "Just spell it the simplest possible way - W-O-O-M."

"There's a B in it, you dope," said the second. "It's spelled W-O-O-M-B."

"You don't have enough letters," objected the third. "I think it ought to be spelled W-O-O-O-M-M-B."

"Nonsense," said the fourth. "It's ridiculous to put in all those letters. Besides, there's a final R. It's W-O-M-B-R-R."

The young lady could stand it no more. Having finished her meal, she approached the other table and said, "Gentlemen, if you'll consult the dictionary, you'll find that the word is spelled W-O-M-B. That's all." And she walked away.

The men gazed after her with astonishment.

"Do you suppose she's right?" asked one.

"How can she be?" said a second. "A slip of a girl like that! I'm sure that never in her whole life has she heard an elephant fart!"
(3:#558)

The Fartress

A maid-servant happened to fart in front of her master, and he became angry, and was going to strike her, but, seeing her white hips, his anger suddenly abated, and he took his pleasure with her. The next day, when he was in his study there was a knock at the door. It was the maid-servant. "What is it? What do you want?" "Please sir, I farted again a little while ago." (7:pg.129)

A boy and a girl were walking along up hill together. All at once the boy detected a disagreeable odor, and asked the girl, "Did you let a fart?" "Of course," she replied; "you don't think I smell like this all the time, do you?!" (30:pg.867)

A young man squiring the Vicar's daughter in his buggy. "As horses will, Stewart's beast, regardless of the lady's presence, relieved itself noisily. 'Really, I am most awfully sorry,' began Stewart stupidly. The Vicar's daughter looked surprised and said, 'O dear! I thought it was the horse.'" (From Kimbo's *Tropical Tales;* Nice, 1925. Pg. 90) (30:pg. 859)

A concert-farter is discovered by an American conductor through the thin wall of a hotel bedroom, and is pushed into world-wide prominence for this art. On the man's first appearance in Boston, as guest soloist, he bows to the audience, enters his little draped kiosk, with a blue spotlight on the center, and presents his instrument. The conductor raps with his baton and gives the signal for the opening tutti, but the soloist does not emit any sound. The conductor raps again, starts over, but again no sound from the soloist. Raps again, begins again, and this time the soloist makes a heroic effort and shits all over the stage. Later, explaining the calamity, he says, "How in hell was I supposed to know you tune the A to 450 in Boston?" (30:pg. 872)

A travelling salesman over taken by night is put up by a Pennsylvania Dutch farmer, and is self-consciously sitting at the table with the whole family eating supper when the farmer lets a tremendous fart. "Do you do this before your children?" asked the shocked traveller. "No," says the farmer; "ve got no rules. Sometimes me first, sometimes dem first." (30:pg.868)

And let us not allow ourselves to forget the almost instinctual and spontaneous reaction to the most frequently told joke of them all: the unexpected sonance of farting; anytime, anywhere.

LAY

One; a stinker. (See FART)

LEGMAN, GERSHON (1917-   )

G. Legman is a specialist in the scholarship of erotica and any denied folklore. In his *Rationale of the Dirty Joke, Series Two*, under the major heading "Scatology" and especially under the subheading of "Crepitation," Mr. Legman's vast knowledge of fartology very quickly becomes rampantly revealed. Some of his philosophically oriented concerns become apparent in the following quotes:

"An excessive interest in crepitation or farting is expressed in jokes, all out of proportion to the actual humor in so minor a physiological activity based on fermentation of undigested starch in the intestine. The fart has been used as the focus for a great deal of

57

the embarrassment felt by the overcivilized as to the natural processes of digestion, and it is ideally suited for this as being only a partial and incorporeal manifestation of the fecal reality underlying." (30:pg.858)

"Jokes about farting must also be an evasive form of scatological abuse of women, since a large proportion of these are particularly concerned with the embarrassment of women in this way..." (30:pg.858)

"None of these jokes seem very funny to ordinary people. To fart-fanciers, however, they are apparently the acme of ethereal humor and Aeolian delight. Whether or not they do it in the bathtub, and 'bite at the bubbles.'" (30:pg.890)

LE PET

This is what the French call a fart. (See CREPITUS)

LE PETOMANE

See PUJOL, JOSEPH.

LET

Fly a rouser; it fly, loose. (See FART)

LIMERICKS

Baart, cart, garter, dart, President Carter, Martin, partin', tart and have a heart: what do all these words have in common?
    Yes, they all rhyme with a most interesting and ancient word: f--t. What a resource for the scatological limerick! Yet out of over a hun-

dred of them I shall only reproduce three.
Happily though, one of them is of epic length.
(Another epic, *The Lyrical Lad from Penn Char-
ter* by Roy Warren West, is mentioned in Legman's *Rationale* (30:pg.872), yet I have never
seen nor heard of a published copy though I
have tried.) The other two poems are included
because of their interesting commentaries by
Douglas, who attempted to put together the
first definitive collection of "dirty" limericks. (I think Legman succeeded...curiously,
I have seen several editions of Legman's
Limerick in the bookstores which exist without
any credit to Mr. Legman whatsoever!)

#740: THE FARTER FROM SPARTA

There was a young fellow from Sparta,
A really magnificent farter,
    On the strength of one bean
    He'd fart God Save the Queen,
And Beethoven's Moonlight Sonata.

He could vary, with proper persuasion,
His fart to suit any occasion.
    He could fart like a flute,
    Like a lark, like a lute,
This highly fartistic Caucasian.

This sparkling young farter from Sparta,
His fart for no money would barter.
    He could roar from his rear
    Any scene from Shakespeare,
Or Gilbert and Sullivan's Mikado.

He'd fart a gavotte for a starter,
And fizzle a fine serenata.
    He could play on his anus
    The Coriolanus:
Oof, boom, er-tum, tootle, yum tah-dah!

He was great in the Christmas Cantata,
He could double-stop fart the Toccata,
    He'd boom from his ass
    Bach's B-Minor Mass,
And in counterpoint, La Traviata.

Spurred on by a very high wager
With an envious German named Bager,
　　He'd proceed to fart
　　The complete oboe part
Of a Haydn Octet in B-Major.

His repertoire ranged from classics to jazz
He achieved new effects with bubbles of gas.
　　With a good dose of salts
　　He could whistle a waltz
Or swing it in razzamatazz.

His basso profundo with timbre so rare
He rendered quite often, with power to spare.
　　But his great work of art,
　　His fortissimo fart,
He saved for the Marche Militaire.

One day he was dared to perform
The William Tell Overture Storm,
　　But naught could dishearten
　　Our spirited Spartan,
For his fart was in wonderful form.

It went off in capital style,
And he farted it through with a smile,
　　Then feeling quite jolly,
　　He tried the finale,
Blowing double-stopped farts all the while.

The selection was tough, I admit,
But it did not dismay him one bit,
　　Then, with ass thrown aloft
　　He suddenly coughed...
And collapsed in a shower of shit.

His bunghole was blown back to Sparta,
Where they buried the rest of our farter,
　　With a gravestone of turds
　　Inscribed with the words:
"To the Fine Art of Farting, A Martyr."

　　He could fart anything
　　From God Save the King

　　From Stravinsky to swing (29)

60

There was a young Royal Marine
Who tried to fart "God Save the Queen."
   When he reached the soprano
    Out came the guano,
And his breeches weren't fit to be seen.
(29#720)

Of this limerick, Norman Douglas had this
comment to make (16:pg.69):

"God Save the Queen": that gives us the approximate date of this gem.

The soprano begins with the stirring words
"Send her victorious," and the muscular strain
involved in producing these high notes may have
led to the disaster. A fit of coughing, or even
laughter, has been known to result in a similar
cataclysm - a distressing state of affairs, if
you happen to be in society at the moment.

The talent of this young Marine, though rare,
is not unique. Visitors to the Paris exhibition
of 1889, if they frequented certain low haunts,
will remember a performer called *"l'homme
petard,"* who achieved wonderful effects on the
same organ. His vocal range was amazing, and
the soprano notes worthy of Tetrazzini. It has
since occurred to me that he may have concealed
about his person the musical instrument called
"petophone," a specimen of which I bought in
Naples many years ago. It is carried in a trousers' pocket and, when squeezed, imitates that
particular vox humana so beautifully that, after a hush of general consternation, it becomes
a great success at dinner parties, diplomatic
receptions, Royal levees, etc.

I should have liked to add a few words on the
guano deposits of Peru and of Saint Paul's
Rocks, but this note is already too long.

There was a young lady of Pinner,
Who drempt that her lover was in her.
   This excited her heart,
    So she let a great fart,
And shit out yesterday's dinner.
(29#729)

Again, Douglas comments:

The muscular contraction provoked by a dream of this nature led to the same result as that described in Limerick #720.

Note the truthfulness of the last line. The accident occurred at night, and if the poet had written 'followed by dinner and luncheon' the meals would have been excreted in their wrong order - a feat which I defy anybody to perform. (16:pg.38)

MARRIAGE

Marriage is obviously the act of being married yet it is listed here because of the interrelated topic: "farting and marriage." For example, folklore has a saying that "the honeymoon is over when the husband begins to fart in the wife's presence." (30:pg.866) And Leslie Fielder, American author, gave us this advice given to him before his marriage: "Be intimate with your wife, but not familiar. When you have to fart in bed, lean your ass over the edge." (19) Jonathan Swift was also one to give freely advice. In his poem *"Strephon and Chloe"* the young bride's parents are advised on what advice to give their young daughter.

Now, Ponder well ye Parents dear;
Forbid your Daughter guzzling Beer:
And, make them ev'ry Afternoon
Forbear their Tea, or drink it soon;
That, e're to Bed they venture up,
They may discharge it ev'ry Sup:

If not; they must in evil Plight
Be often forc'd to rise at Night;
Keep them to wholesome food confin'd,
Not let them taste what causes Wind;
(Tis this the Sage of Samos means,
Forbidding his Disciples Beans)
O, think what Evils must ensue;
Miss Moll the Jade will burn it blue:
And, when she once hath got the Art,
She cannot help it for her Heart;
But, out it flies, ev'n when she meets
Her Bridegroom in the Wedding Sheets.
Carminative and Diuretick,
Will damp all Passion Sympathetick:
And Love such Nicety requires,
One blast will put out all his Fires.
Since Husbands get behind the Scene,
The Wife should study to be clean;
Nor give the smallest Room to guess
The Time when wants of Nature press;
But, after Marriage, practise more
Decorum than she did before;
To keep her Spouse deluded still,
And make him fancy what she will. (42:lines
115-144)

Here is a tale that was written down around
1535 and it tells a story of a woman who followed well the advise recorded in the last four
lines of Swift's above quoted passage. It tells
of how her husband discovered her deception.
The story is entitled "Of the merchant that
made a wager with his lord" and it goes like
this:

A certain merchant, before his lord that he
was subject unto, among other things praised
his wife and said that he never heard her let
a fart. Whereat the lord marveled and said it
was impossible, and so laid and ventured a supper with the merchant that before three months
were ended, he should hear her let a fart or
twain. On the morrow, the lord came to the merchant and borrowed fifty crowns, the which he
promised truly to repay again within eight

days after. The merchant right sore against his will lent it, and thoughtfully abode till the day of payment was come, and then he went to his lord and required his money.

The lord, making as though he had more need than before, desired the merchant to lend him another fifty crowns, and promised to pay all within a month. And although the good man denied it long, yet for fear least he should lose the first sum, with much grudging he lent him the other fifty crowns, and so went home to his house right heavy and sorrowful in his mind. Thus thinking and dreading divers things, he passed many nights away without sleep. And as he lay waking, he heard his wife now and then rap out farts.

At the month's end, the lord sent for the merchant and asked him if he never since heard his wife let a fart. The merchant acknowledging his folly, answered thus: "Forsooth, sir, if I should for every fart pay a supper, all my goods and lands would not suffice thereto." After which answer, the lord paid the merchant his money and the merchant paid the supper. (47)

MANURE GATHERING

The days of manure gathering are finished in this section of the world but the way our contemporary energy problems are daily discussed and worried over I think that no one would be too surprised to find people taking stock in a wooded, well trodded country path or a city mounted patrolman's route. A day's hard work in gathering manure is worth several days of warmth during a cold winter. The quote here shows how a good base in fartology can help these neo-manure gatherers of tomorrow. The "joke" that follows tells of how this (shitty) business can get when it isn't.

"The shrewd manure gatherer knew also that cows and horses frequently give certain premon-

itory signs before they do the deed. There is
a perceptible hesitation in the jaunty stride,
a slight hanching of the back, a characteristic
restlessness in the visible part of the organ
involved. Unfortunately, these signs were not
always reliable, since on occasion they turned
out to be over elaborate preambles to an absolutely noncollectable puff of wind. However, an
animal who went through such maneuvers, we all
knew, bore diligent watching." (35a)

A man buys a horse and goes into the horse-
manure business. A friend finds him sitting
backwards on the horse, holding its tail in the
air and examining its anus worriedly. "Business
is terrible," he explains; "I'm feeding this
bastard oats at 40¢ a quart for two weeks now,
and all he does is fart: 'Foof! foof!' A man
can't live on promises!" (30:pg.887)

MONTAIGNE, MICHEL DE (1533-1592)

The *Autobiography of Michel de Montaigne* calls
chapter number 6 "The Discreet Business of Marriage." Under this heading he engages the reader
in a philosophically oriented discussion upon
free will. Thus he has this to say about farts:

"To vindicate the omnipotence of our will,
Saint Augustine alleges that he knew a man who
commanded his behind to produce as many farts as
he wanted, and his commentator Vives goes him
one better with another example of his own time,
of farts arranged to suit the tone of verses
pronounced to their accompaniment; but all this
does not really argue any pure obedience in this
organ; for is there any that is ordinarily more
indiscreet or tumultuous? Besides, I know one so
turbulent and unruly, that for forty years it
has kept his master farting with a constant and
unremitting wind and compulsion, and is thus
taking him to his death. And would God I knew
only from the history books how many times our
stomach, by refusing one single fart, brings us

66

to the gates of a very anguished death; and
that the Emperor who gave us the liberty to
fart anywhere had given us the power to." (32)

(See also ST. AUGUSTINE, VIVES, EMPEROR CLAUDIUS)

MORE, THOMAS (1478-1535)

Thomas More had the good sense to give us
this bit of advice, but the scoundrel went a-
head and wrote it in Latin, thereby saving
only the educated and the elite. Thanks to
Harrington, though, it has been translated for
all of us commoners.

"To break a little wind,
    sometime ones life doth save,
For want of vent behind,
    some folk their ruine have:
A powre it hath therefore,
    of life, and death expresse:
A king can cause no more,
    a cracke doth do no lesse."

The word *Cracke* is defined in a footnote
as *ventris crepitus*. (41)

MYTHOLOGY

Indeed, farts have their place in the mythology of all cultures. Here is a sampling from
Thompson's *Motif-Index of Folk Literature:*

D 2063.5 Magic Discomfort: continued breaking
        wind.
G 93 Cannibal breaks wind as means of attack.
G 303.6.2.15.1 Devil causes boy to make noise
            of breaking wind after he has
            stolen bushel of corn to pay
            for shoes.
F 451.3.13.3 Dwarf breaks wind so hard he cap-
            sizes canoes.
G 269.21.1 Witches causes person to break wind
            in presence of others. (43)

NAD

A Sanskrit term signifying "music heard from no apparent source," it is a phenomenon that frequently occurs in both mysticism and fartology. The "music of the spheres" which played a role in the early science of Pythagoras and later Kepler appears to be related.

OLD FART

See POPE PAUL.

PEELE, GEORGE (1556-1596)

George Peele was an Elizabethan dramatist and ne'er-do-well (so claims Legman) who died around 1596. An English jestbook has this to say about him:

George was upset with some lady at a banquet so for revenge "as she put out her arme to take the Capon, George sitting by her, yerks out a huge fart, which made all the company in a maze, one looking upon the other, yet they knew it came that way. Peace, quoth George, and jogs her on the elbow, I will say it was I. At which all the Company fell into huge laughter, shee into a fretting fury, vowing never she should sleep quietly till she was revenged of George his wrong done unto her: and so in great chase left her company." (30:pg.859)

PET-EN-GUELUTE

This is the French way of saying "fart-in-

the-face." It is included here because of my
conviction that many readers will at some time
in their lives find themselves in a situation
for which the exclamation of this French phrase
will be appropriate. My own time came upon writing this entry. (30:vol.2)

PETOMANIAC

This term is used to describe a person who
farts a great deal. For an interesting discussion of this see FREQUENCY. A petomaniac is
sometimes merely referred to as a *farter*. (personal communication)

PETOPHONE

A petophone is any devise that is used to produce the sound of farting - other than the anus,
that is. Allow me to quote from Dr. Caryle F.
MacIntyre's *That Immortal Garland* (M.S. 1942)
page 1:

"If Reginald had been clever he would have
procured a petophone which he could have used
in conversation. Gallantly he could have assured
any old lady, 'Be quiet, your ladyship, and
they'll think I did it!'" (30:pg.859)

PETS DE NONNE

These French soufflé fritters are made with
choux pastry. After the fritters have been dried
and drained, they are filled with various creams
or jams. They should be made to approximate the
size of walnuts.
Their invention is credited to an anonymous
nun of the abbey of Marmonfier along the Loire.
And although it is known that *"soupirs de nonne"*
(=nun's sigh) was derived to evade the *lower*
form *"pet de nonne"* (=nun's fart) the derivation

of the latter term is unknown. (20a&41e)

PHEROMONE

An odor secreted by an individual that influences the behavior of another individual by stimulating a physiological or behavioral response from other animals of the same species is called a "pheromone." (45)

"POO-POO" CUSHIONS

This is the same thing as a "petophone." See PETOPHONE.

POPE PAUL

An example of an "old fart." (personal communication)

POSTERIOR FLATUS

A synonym for the noun fart. It takes the word "flatus" and gives it *both location and direction*. (See FLATUS) (41)

PUJOL, JOSEPH (1857-1945)

Joseph Pujol was that wonderful man known better as *"Le Petomane."* He could fart at will as long and as loud as he pleased, so he devoted his life to it: he became an artist.
The stories of how he discovered his gift while swimming, of how he could impress his friends and how they encouraged him to enter into the theater, of how he got sued for farting freely and many more true tales can all be found in a delightful little book entitled, *Le Petomane*, his definitive biography, penned by

his eldest son Louis-Baptiste Pujol. (33)
Rather than attempt to print the entire book here, I have chosen only two passages; the first being a recollection of a fellow performer, a singer who used his ordinary voice, Yvette Guilbert; the second being a fantasy written about Le Petomane in 1893 by E. Grenet-Dancourt.

At the Moulin Rouge I [Guilbert] heard the most extraordinary outbursts of laughter, the hilarity was at times almost hysterical. This is how it started. One day Zidler was visited by a sad, pale faced man who told him he was a "phenomenon" and that his gift would become the talk of Paris.

"And what is your gift?"

"Well, you see, sir," his visitor explained in all seriousness, "I have a breathing arse-hole..."

"Oh! yes?" Zidler said in his cold, deadpan way. The other continued as if he were a professor giving instruction.

"You see, sir, my anus is of such elasticity that I can open and shut it at will."

"So what?"

"So thanks to this providential function I can absorb any quantity of liquid I may be given..."

"What's that?" said Zidler. "You drink through your backside? What can I offer you?" he went on ceremoniously.

"A large basin of water if you will."

"Mineral water?"

"No, thank you, ordinary water please."

When the basin was brought the man took off his trousers, revealing a hole in his pants at the necessary place. Then seating himself on the basin, which was filled to the brim, he emptied it and refilled it in no time at all.

Zidler then said that a slight smell of sulphur spread through the room.

"I see, so you manufacture Enghien water!"

The man gave him a little smile.

"Ah, that's not all, sir...once I've been rinsed out in this way, if I may so put it, I

can expel an almost infinite quantity of odour-
less gas - and that is the basis of my gift -
you see, the principle of intoxication..."

"Just a minute," Zidler interrupted, "let's
keep it to simple facts. You're telling me you
can fart..."

"If you like to put it that way," the other
conceded, "but the unique thing about my act is
the deep range of sound I can produce."

"You mean you sing through your backside."

"Well...yes."

"Right. Go ahead. I'm listening."

"First the tenor...one, next the baritone...
two, now the bass...three...the light voice...
four and the vocaliser...five."

Zidler now completely captivated cried out:
"And the one you call the mother-in-law?"

"Here she is," said Le Petomane.

And on that Zidler engaged him. On the bill-
boards it read:

Every evening from 8 to 9
LE PETOMANE
The only one who pays no author's royalties

Zidler put him in the Elephant in the garden.
They fell over themselves to hear him and the
laughter, shouting, women's shrieking and the
whole hysterical din could be heard a hundred
yards away from the Moulin Rouge. When Le Petomane saw his public gripped in this way he shout-
ed, "All together, then, one two three..." They
joined him in chorus and the whole house was
convulsed.

That Sunday Le Petomane's take was a thousand
louis. (33:pg.8-12)

E. GRENET-DANCOURT
Le Ventomane
Comic monologue by X...member of the
Comedie-Francaise

Ollendorff, 1893

All my life I shall never forget the first time
I saw him or the second time I heard him...aston-

74

ishing...marvellous...sublime! Never had I been carried so high into the ether of art...never, never, never...the moment he came on a great silence descended...looking round with a sweet melancholy - almost as if dreaming - he took in the house - and what an audience he had! The nobility from the two Foubourgs and every single literary, artistic and fashionable personality there might be in Paris...(Seriously) Quality will always draw a crowd and even the most blase display at times a determination to immerse themselves once more in the ideal and to breathe another air than that of every day... the Master thus welcomed bowed slightly, put his hands on his knees and with the nonchalance of a lord, smilingly opened his - er - hum!...and began. A thrill of excitement ran through the auditorium. To begin with a sweet song like that of a swallow...something gentle, timid and tender like the sigh of a young girl...of a young girl who has known unhappiness...a breath, a mere nothing...Then all of a sudden the note changes and grows - the poem becomes epic... hesitant and weak at the start, the voice grows firmer and stronger...no longer does it caress, it threatens! Impetuously it growls, thunders, explodes, groans - cyclone - hurricane - tempest! Lightning strikes in the tortured firmament and whilst in the distance a warning gun is fired, distractedly under our very eyes the thunder growls to excess...it was terrifying... never have I seen such a storm...a dry storm, of course, but then they are the worst...but hist!...listen...calm has returned and the gentle song of rocking waves mounts once more in the air...oh! harmony...harmony...harmony!!! And so it went on for two hours...we were all of us there hanging on the Master's lips, feverish, gasping - and while the men sought to hide their emotion by biting their moustaches - beneath the velvets, silks and lace the women's breasts heaved tumultuously...as for me, I was crying no longer having just enough strength left to applaud the man who was making my tears

flow...at last he stood up and looking down
once more on the audience with his sweet dreaming melancholy, took his farewell and disappeared...I went home, my head on fire, and before going to sleep tried myself to reproduce
what I had just heard...nothing, nothing, nothing...The next morning I began again - the
same result...indeed even after fifteen days,
I was not a step further on...not a thing...
others in my place would have been equally dis-
couraged...it's simply not fair...when one has
a fixed idea and above all when one feels one
has something in the wind...one fine morning,
taking my courage in both hands, I sought out
the Master and asked him to instruct me in his
method, to give me lessons...it's a difficult
career, he told me straight away, it's rough
going...not too much competition till now, young
man, but the going is tough...and he listed the
vexations and difficulties...he had himself
started very young indeed and it had only been
by hard work, perseverance and will power that
he had succeeded in making a name for himself
and an enviable situation...he saw that I had
the physical means to hand but that was not e-
nough...other qualities were necessary, nay
indispensable...finally he pointed out that
parents often have preconceived ideas and that
perhaps my family intended me for some other
profession than that of artist. Nevertheless
five minutes later he was giving me my first
lesson...oh! how difficult it is to start...
I had no voice...I was lacking in voice...feel-
ing - yes - plenty of that, gesture and warmth
but no vocal ability...I was in the pit of des-
pair...but he restored my battered courage...
what's the good of getting angry? he said...
have patience...it will come...and it's true,
it did...after six months of work, twelve hours
a day, the voice is there...still a little thin
in volume...but of quality...so I am no longer
an amateur...and what does it matter if the
sharps and flats still bother me a little? I'm
not doing badly...I've already tried it out in

one or two drawing rooms - among friends of
course...and it's been a success...a nice little success...well mothers with marriageable
daughters have started giving me the eye...and
even my parents - well, they're actually proud
of me these days...so let's get on with it,
shall we? I'll give you a little sample of
what I can do...you'd like it? I have a bit of
a cold so you must be indulgent...Right!...
Hm!...It's a question of not being taken short
...(after a pause) I've got it (bowing grac-
iously at the audience). By the side of a lake,
one summer evening...soft breezes (he gets into
position, one hand on his thigh, the other
raised to the sky). Here we go...(after a moment his face clouds over with the look of a
man who has just suffered a totally unexpected
accident and straightening up he holds himself
tightly in) I *have* been taken short...goodbye!
(He pivots round and goes off running at full
speed.) (33:pg.90-95)

RABELAIS, FRANCOIS (1494-1553)

As one would expect, Rabelais frequently has a great deal of fartistic knowledge to bestow upon his readers. Thus it comes as no surprise that as Gargantua "blew a fat fart," Pantagruel is visiting the infamous Library of St. Victor in which he finds "most magnificent, especially for certain books which he discovered in it." Some of the books he finds there include:

The Art of Farting Decently in Public Tartaret, on methods of shitting. (II,vii, 187-90)

Still later, we find these two "extracting farts from a dead donkey and selling them at five pence a yard." (39)

RALLYING

Often, when the unexpected sound of a fart is

delivered, to obscure the embarrassment that is sure to be draped upon its author, the farter has numerous phrases to rally the fart so as to displace the inevitable humor on to the phrase used, rather than the fart itself. Here is a brief sampling.

1. "You shut your mouth, nobody asked you!" (30:pg.876)
2. "If you're going to talk, I'll be quiet..." (30:pg.867)
3. "The Voice of Destiny!" (30:pg.867)
4. "Pardon my Southern accent..." (30:pg.867)
5. "Who pulled your chin?" (30:pg.876)
6. "Your announcer: Oscar Poot!" (30:pg.876)
7. "Did an Angel speak?" (46)
8. "Beans for breakfast?" (30:pg.876)
9. Or one may merely slap one's buttocks in a scolding way. (30:pg.876)
10. "Opps, I stepped on a duck!" (Thus spake Rodney Dangerfield in the 1980 movie *Caddy-Shack.*)
11. "Now here this, now hear this...," and then comes the fart. (6a:pg.181)
12. "Pardon my fartin'" (personal communication)

RIDDLES

Fart riddles! They do exist. Here is a sampling from days gone by.

1. "Demaunde: Who was he that lette the fyrst farte at rome? That was the arse." (*The Demaundes Joyous:* 1511)

2. To all around me Mirth I make,
       tho seldom spend my Pelf;
   And what so'ere I chance to say,
       I always shame my self.
   I'm usher'd into Company
       of those of best Degree,
   Who all congradulating Bow,
       when 'ere they know 'tis me.

Yet who so 'ere me entertains,
   turns usually a Sneaker,
Tho' of the commons House ('tis true)
   I once was Mr. Speaker.
And tho I'm chose no Member now,
   I often fill the Chair
But very seldom come into 't
   if th' Speaker be not there.
I live to so great length of Age,
   I die for want of Breath,
And yet when 'ere I hap to die,
   I sing before my Death.
(Thesaurus Aenigmaticus: 1725-6:pg.35)

3. Because I am by Nature *blind,*
   I wisely chuse to walk *behind;*
   However, to avoid Disgrace,
   I let no Creature see my *Face.*
   My Words are few, but spoke with *Sense:*
   And yet my *speaking* give Offense:
   Or, if to *whisper* I presume,
   The Company will fly the Room.
   By all the world I am *oppress't,*
   And my *Oppression* gives them *Rest.*

   It is at this point that we find ourselves
with the uncontrollable urge to blurt out the
question, "Who am I?" - true to the genre of
this kind of riddle. Yet the poem continues...

   By Thousands I am *sold* and *bought,*
   Who neither get, nor lose a Groat;
   For none, alas, by me can gain,
   By those who give me *greatest Pain.*
   (Line 13-16)

   In me, Detractors seek to find
   Two Vices of a diff'rent Kind:
   I'm too *profuse* some Cens'rers cry,
   And all I get, I *let it fly:*
   While others give me many a Curse,
   Because too close I hold my Purse.
   (Lines 23-28) (From Jonathan Swift's *"Be-
cause I am by Nature blind.")* (28&42)

80

SAINT AUGUSTINE (354-430)

St. Augustine was an early Algerian church-
father who in the middle of his life gave up
the life of a pagan and a lot of things that
go with that kind of life to become devoted to
the Christian belief system. Thus he tells us
in Book xiv, chapter 24 of his *City of God*
about a man who could fart at will. "There are
those that can break wind backward so artfully
that you would think they sung." See also
MONTAINGE.

S. B. D.

Silent But Deadly farts, like "sliders," cannot be heard. They make themselves known by
their powerfully odiferous effect. (Personal
communication)
Remember what "Bugs" Baer once said? "God put
the stink in a fart for guys who are hard of

hearing ... and to catch the bastards that try
to sneak out those silent sneakers." (30:pg.863)

SCHOOL OF SALERNO

This eleventh century school was founded in
the Gulf of Naples by four well-known doctors -
a Greek, an Italian, a Jew and an Arab.
It appears that once the Crusaders came here
to alleviate the pains of "wind held in." The
school's Health Code was that

To release certain winds is considered almost
            a crime.
Yet those who suppress them risk dropsy, con-
            vulsion,
Vertigo and frightful colics.
These are too often the unhappy outcome
Of a sad discretion. (33:pg.54)

SCREAMERS

Farts that are very loud and high pitched
speak out their existence and are therefore
called "screamers." Odor rarely accompanies
them.

SENGAI (1750-1837) (See cover)

This Japanese artist once painted a picture
entitled "The Teaching of the Law of a Hundred
Days," 'hundred days' meaning always, everyday.
It is, in fact, a drawing of a boy bent over
farting and is "remarkable in that it unites
the very lowest with the very highest, and when
this is done we have humor, poetry, and the
whole Truth." (7:pg.249)

"The picture shows the beatific pleasure of
the farter, perhaps a child, and his helping the
farting with his right hand stretched to the
rear. From the Freudian point of view we must

say that farting is a sexual pleasure, and a sexual symbol. But more profoundly, the universe is God's fart. Most of us find that it stinks, and hold our noses. We should, instead, take a deep breath of it." (7:pg.249)

The characters scribbled along the side say:

"Now then! Eat away!
Drink up your tea!"

SLIDERS

Farts that are purposely released in such a manner as to "slide" out noiselessly are called (appropriately) *sliders*. Let us quote Mr. Legman (30:pg.864) who appears to be an expert on sliders:

"In practice...the individual, anxious to avoid noisy farting and offense, surreptitiously leans on ('tilts') or draws open one buttock to relax the sphincter and allow the pent-up fermentational gas of the intestine to ooze out quietly. Though generally successful, this unfortunately sometimes has only the effect of changing the timbre of the note achieved, bringing it into a lower diapason in which might only have been an embarrassing 'screamer' emerges as a disasterous 'fizzle.' Let us draw the curtain mercifully here."

SNORKLE

See BATHTUBS.

SWIFT, JONATHAN (1667-1745)

The use of scatological literary devices throughout the works of Jonathan Swift has caused much controversy amongst literary scholars. Many have viewed such devices as just plain dirty and disgusting. Now that more and more people are becoming dirty and disgusting, Swift's more "obscene" works are becoming favorites among people of all intellectual realms. Here is a sample taken from his poem *The Lady's Dressing Room*. Also included here is his poem *The Problem*. Other examples can be found under the headings MARRIAGE and RIDDLES.

His foul Imagination links
Each Dame he sees with all her Stinks:
And, if unsav'ry Odours fly,
Conceives a lady standing by. (42:lines 121-4)

The Problem (1699)

    Did ever Problem thus perplex,
Or more employ the Female Sex?
So sweet a Passion, who would think,
Jove ever form'd to make a Stink?
The Ladies vow and swear they'll try,
Whether it be a Truth or Lie.

    Love's Fire, it seems, like inward Heat,
Works in my Lord by Stool and Sweat:
Which brings a Stink from ev'ry Pore
And from behind, and from before:
Yet, what is wonderful to tell it,
None but the favorite Nymph can smell it.
But now to solve the nat'ral Cause
By sober philosophic Laws:
Whether all Passions when in Ferment,
Work out, as Anger does in Vermin;
So, when a Weazel you torment,
You find his Passion by his Scent.
We read of Kings, who in a Fright,
Though on a Throne would fall to shite.
Beside all this deep Scholars know,
That the main String of Cupid's Bow,
Once on a Time was an Asses gut,
Now to a nobler Office put,
By Favour or Desert preferr'd
From giving Passage to a Turd;
But still, though fix'd among the Stars,
Doth sympathize with human Arse,

Thus, when you feel an hard-bound Breech,
Conclude Love's Bow-string at full stretch,
'Till the kind Looseness comes, and then
Conclude the Bow relax'd again.

And now the Ladies all are bent
To try the great Experiment,
Ambitious of a Regent's Heart,
Spread all their Charms to catch a Fart!
Watching the first unsav'ry Wind,
Some ply before, and some behind.
My Lord on Fire amidst the Dames,
Farts like a Laurel in the Flames.
The Fair approach the speaking Part,
To try the back Way to his Heart.
For, as when we a Gun discharge,
Although the Bore be ne'er so large,
Before the Flame from Muzzle burst,
Just at the Breech it flashes first:
So from my Lord his Passion broke,
He farted first, and then he spoke.

The Ladies vanish in the Smother,
To confer Notes with one another:
And now they all agree to name
Whom each one thought the happy Dame.
Quoth Neal, what e'er the rest may think,
I'm sure 'twas I that smelt the Stink.
You smelt the Stink! By God, you lie,
Quoth Ross, for I'll be sworn 'twas I.
Ladies, quoth Levens, pray forbear,
Let's not fall out, we all had Share;
And, by the most I can discover,
My Lord's an universal Lover. (42)

THIEBEAU, ANGELE

A farting imposter, this infamous *la femme-petomane* tried to ride upon the fame of the natural fartist Joseph Pujol (better known as Le Petomane) by producing fraudulent sounds with a pair of bellows hidden under her skirt. (33)

THOREAU, HENRY (1817-1862)

Henry Thoreau once wrote, "I was determined to know beans." See BEANS.

TOBA SŌJŌ (1053-1114)

"In the later part of the age, many humorous picture scrolls were made, one of the first and best being by Bishop Toba, a monk of the Tendai Sect who lived in Toba (Yamashiro). His age was

one of political, social, artistic, and religious langour and decadence, a preparation for
the Saprtan Kamakura Period to follow. Toba
seems to have been far from unlike the witty
and jovial monks of the European Middle Ages.
He was the ninth child of Minamoto Takakuni,
the author of *Ima wa Mukashi*. His four scrolls
of *Chojugiga*, 'Bird and Beast Comical Pictures'
are now world-famous, though recently some cri-
tics have assessed them lower, as art, than
formerly."

"Another scroll-picture attributed to Toba is
the *Shukyuzu*, 'Stinking Fart Picture.' This is
what is known as a *kachi-e*, which seems to mean
Competition Picture, or Winning Picture. The
retired Emperor Enyu, who died in 1084, seven
years after his abdication, suffered from hypo-
chondria, and when all other medicines and mag-
ical arts had failed it was suggested that he
needed to be made to laugh, so Bishop Toba
kindly obliged with the above pictures of men
and women farting. This may seem a little on
the vulgar side, but is not the good Bishop
trying to save the world, and in a far more
effective way than the Bishop in *Les Miserables?*"
(7:pg.287)

TOILETS

Great ideas are often preserved in public
toilets. Here is one of them:

"Here I sit broken hearted,
    Paid a dime and only farted." (46)

TORNGARSUK

The Eskimo Indians believe in a being called
Torngarsuk.

"They don't all agree about his form or aspect. Some say he has no form at all; others
describe him as a great bear, or as a great man

87

with one arm, or as small as a finger. He is
immortal, but might be killed by the interven-
tion of the god Crepitus." (See CREPITUS) (27)

Crantz, in his book *The History of Greenland*
had this to say about Torngarsuk:

"He is immortal, and yet might be killed, if
anyone breaks wind in a house where witchcraft
is carrying on." (14)

TROMBONA, LA

"When he called to his wife, across the courtyard from his workshop, to fetch him the wine
jug, his affectionate love call was the envy of
all hen-ridden males who lacked his gall and the
burly framework with which to back it up. *'Ei,
brutta puttana sganghersata, quando me la porti
quella benedetta bottiglia?!* What ho! You ugly,
unhinged whore, when are you going to bring me
that blessed bottle?'

"At the sound of her darling's voice, she
emerged belligerently from the kitchen door, a
mountainous, shapeless mass draped in a heavy,
loose, and voluminous woolen dress that, so far
as the neighbors could tell, had not been changed
in a quarter of a century. It was gathered somewhere above the navel with a knitted bright red
scarf and extended to the ground. As she wad-
dled across the yard, her heavy breasts swaying
rhythmically from side to side, she chewed in-
cessantly on pumpkin seeds - of which she had
an inexhaustible supply - and looked intently
and rather menacingly toward the shop. When she
approached her mate, whom she dearly loved, she
held out the wine jug and addressed him in language as vigorous and original as his own. *'Ecco
la tua puttana, brutto bastardo pidocchioso.
Bevi e affoga, porce ghiottone.'* Here comes your
whore, you ugly, louse-ridden bastard. Drink and
drown yourself, you gluttonous swine.

"As she handed him the bottle, he hoisted his
heavy-booted foot in the general direction of her

belly. It was a wholly futile thrust, for she
had learned by experience that by stooping
slightly forward and grabbing his foot in mid-
air, she could avoid his trecherous blow. When
she had him thus helpless in her strong grip,
she would grin and spit, then throw his boot to
the ground and retreat, laughing like a witch.
As she reached the middle of the courtyard she
would turn her rear toward him, bend slightly
forward, look over her shoulder and wink af-
fectionately, as she let him have a blast so
terrific that it fanned her skirt into a complete circle. Her talent for releasing such
thunderclaps at will was so amazing that she
was everywhere known as *La Trombona*. (35a)

TWAIN, MARK (1835-1910)

Author of *1601 Conversation as It Was...By
the Social Fireside in the Time of the Tudors*.
One of this story's main concerns is to discover the authorship of a "stench so all-pervading and immortal."
   It was written in the summer of 1876 when
Twain was just finishing *Tom Sawyer* and about
to begin *Huckleberry Finn*. "If there is a de-
cent word findable in it," he once wrote to a
Cleveland librarian, "it is because I over-looked
it."
   Influenced by one of his favorite books,
Pepy's Diary, he meant it as a letter to his
close friend Rev. Joseph Twichell of Asylum
Hill Congregational Church in Hartford, Connect-
icut. Another friend, David Gray, happened to
see the piece before it was mailed. He said,
"Print it and put your name to it Mark. You have
never done a greater piece of work than that."
Later, John Hay, soon to become Sec. of State,
somehow saw the work (1880) and had four copies
put out in pamphlet form. He thought it "a most
exquisite bit of Old English morality." It has
been circulated privately, through many editions,
ever since.

Yesternight toke her majesty ye queene a fan-
tasie such as she sometimes hath, and had to her
closet certain that doe write playes, bokes, and
such like, these being my lord Bacon, his worship Sir Walter Raleigh, Mr. Ben Jonson, and ye
child Francis Beaumonte, which being but sixteen,
hath yet turned his hand to ye doing of yet
Lattin masters into our Englishe tong, with
grete discretion and much applaus. Also came
with these ye famous Shaxpur. A right straunge
mixing truly of mighty blode with mean, ye more
in especial since ye queenes grace was present,
as likewise these following, to wit: Ye Duchess
of Bilgewater, twenty-two yeres of age; ye
Countess of Granby, twenty-six; her doter, ye
Lady Helen, fifteen; as also these two maides
of honor, to wit, Ye Lady Margery Boothby, sixty-
five, and ye Lady Alice Dilberry, turned seventy,
she being two yeres ye queenes graces elder.

I being her majesty's cup-bearer, had no
choice but to remaine and beholde, rank forgot,
and ye high holde converse with ye low as upon
equal termes, a grete scandal did ye world heare
thereof.

In ye heat of ye talk it befel yt one did
breake wind, yielding an exceeding mightie and
distresfull stink, whereat all did laugh full
sore, and then –

YE QUEENE.– Verily in mine eight and sixty
yeres have I not heard the fellow to this fart.
Meseemeth, by ye grete sound and clamour of it,
it was male; yet ye belly it did lurk behinde
shoulde now fall lean and flat against ye spine
of him yt hath bene delivered of so stately and
so vaste a bulk, whereas ye guts of them yt doe
quiffsplitters bear, stand comely still and
rounde. Prithee let ye author confess ye offspring. Will my Lady Alice testify?

LADY ALICE.– Good your grace, an' I had room for
such a thunderbust within mine ancient bowels,
'tis not in reason I could discharge ye same
and live to thank God for yet. He did choose
handmaid so humble whereby to shew his power.

Nay, 'tis not I yet have broughte forth this
rich o'er-mastering fog, this fragrant gloom,
so pray ye seeke ye further.

YE QUEENE.- Mayhap Lady Margery hath done ye
companie this favor?

LADY MARGERY.- So please you madam, my limbs
are feeble with ye weighte and drouth of five
and sixty winters, and it behoveth yt I be tender unto them. In ye good providence of God, an'
I had contained this wonder, forsoothe wolde I
have gi'en ye whole evening of my sinking life
to ye dribbling of it forth, with trembling and
uneasy soul, not launched it sudden in its
matchless might, taking my own life with vio-
lence, rending my weak frame like rotten rags.
It was not I, your Majesty.

YE QUEENE.- O' God's name who hath favored us?
Hath it come to pass yt a fart shall fart *itself?* Not such a one as this, I trow. Young
Master Beaumont - but no; 'twould have wafted
him to heaven like down of goose's boddy. 'Twas
not ye little Lady Helen - nay, ne're blush,
my child; thoul't tickle thy tender maidenhedde
with many a mousie-squeak before thou learnest
to blow a harricane like this. Was't you, my
learned and ingenious Jonson?

JONSON.- So fell a blast hath ne'er mine ears
saluted, nor yet a stench so all-pervading and
immortal. 'Twas not a novice did it, good your
majesty, but one of veteran experience - else
hadde he failed of confidence. In sooth it was
not I.

YE QUEENE.- My Lord Bacon?

LORD BACON.- Not from my leane entrailes hath
this prodigy burst forth, so please your grace.
Naught doth so befit ye grete as grete perfor-
mance; and haply shall ye finde yet is not from
mediocrity this miracle hath issued.

(Tho' ye subject be but a fart, yet will this
tedious sink of learning pondrously phillosophize.

Meantime did the foul and deadly stink per-
vade all places to that degree, yt never smelt
I ye like, yet dare I not to leave ye presence,
albeit I was like to suffocate.)

YE QUEENE.- What saith ye worshipful Master
Shaxpur?

SHAXPUR.- In the great hand of God I stand - and
so proclaim mine innocence. Though ye sinless
hosts of heaven had foretold ye coming of this
most desolating breath, proclaiming it a work
of uninspired man, its quaking thunders, its
firmament-clogging rottenness his own achieve-
ment in due course of nature, yet had not I
believed it; but had said the pit itself hath
furnished forth the stink, and heaven's artillery hath shook the globe in admiration of it.

(Then there was a silence, and each did turn
him toward the worshipful Sir Walter Raleigh,
that browned, embattled, bloody swash-buckler
who rising up did smile, and simpering say) -

SIR WALTER.- Most gracious Majesty, 'twas I that
did it; but indeed it was so poor and frail a
note, compared with such as I am wont to fur-
nish, yt in sooth, I was ashamed to call the
weakling mine in so august a presence. It was
nothing - less than nothing, madam - I did it
but to clear my nether throat; but had I come
prepared, then haid I delivered something
worthy. Bear with me, please your grace, till I
can make amends.

(Then delivered he himself of such a godless
and rock-shivering blast that all were fain to
stop their ears, and following it did come so
dense and foul a stink that that which went before did seem a poor and trifling thing beside
it. Then saith he, feigning that he blushed and
was confused, *'I perceive that I am weak to-day,
and cannot justice do unto my powers;'* and sat
him down as who should say, *'There, it is not
much; yet he that hath an arse to spare, let
him follow that, an think he can.'* By God, and

92

were ye Queene, I would e'en tip this swaggering braggard out o' the court, and let him air his grandeurs and break his intolerable wind before ye deaf and such as soffocation pleaseth.)

Later, Sir Walter is briefly referred to as "ye damned windmill!"

VERVILLE, BEROALDE DE

Beroalde de Verville wrote a book around 1610 of which the following passage is a loose translation. His book was entitled *Le Moyen de Parvenir* (The Way of Succeeding), and the passage can be found in chapter 7, "Couplet." Verville states: "The original of this came out of the cabinet of our Ambroise Pare," the greatest French physician and surgeon of the preceeding century. (30:pg.884)

"The Lord of Lierne, a French gentleman, went to bed with a courtesan in Rome. As chaste courtesans well know their business, she had procured some little pellicules which had been filled with scented air through the skill of perfumers. Having a supply of these wares and holding the gentleman in her arms, the good Imperia allowed herself to be loved. To add an edge to the fondling and to draw her lover more closely, the lady took one of the pellicules in her hand and burst it, thus making the audible sound of a

fart. On hearing this the gentleman withdrew
his head from the bed to give himself air.
'It's not what you think,' she said, 'you must
hear before being afraid.' Thus persuaded he
received an agreeable odour quite contrary to
what he had expected and which he savoured with
pleasure. This having been repeated a number of
times, he enquired of the lady if such winds
proceeded from her considering that they smelt
so good and given the fact that similar winds
emanating from the lower portions of French
ladies were stinking and abominable. To this
she replied with a little frisky philosophy to
the effect that Italian ladies, due to the
aromatic food and to the use of odoriferous
articles produced their quintessence in the
lower regions as if it were a neck of a retort.
'In truth,' he replied, 'our own ladies fart
in a quite different way.'"
    "It so happened that after some more musketry
and on account of withholding her wind for too
long, Imperia farted naturally, substantially
and at length. The Frenchman diligently stuck
his nose under the sheets in order to appre-
hend the good odour which he wished to savour to
the full. But he was deceived; he received
through his nose a stench of barnyard proportions. 'Oh! my dear lady,' he said, 'what have
you done?' She answered, 'My lord, I was but
paying you a compliment to remind you of your
own country.'"

VIVES, JUAN LOUIS (1492-1540)

    What Vives, the Spanish humanist and contem-
porary of Rabelais, actually said in his 16th
century commentary (1522) on St. Augustine was:

    "There was an one, a Germane, about Maximilian's
court, and his son Phillip's, that would have
rehearsed any verse whatsoever with his taile."
(30:pg.871)

AFTERWORD: *By Jim Patterson*

Our story begins in one of the great monasteries of China. Here lived Moo Kao, a nun, who toiled the lighter hours of a day in a kitchen preparing food and cleaning dishes for the warrior monks who resided in the monastery. Moo Kao had a visitation one night; it was in a dream. A great fiery dragon descended from the darkness and so mounted her, to which she gave herself willingly, believing that she was now truly blessed. Some three quarters of a year later, Moo Kao realized she could no longer stay. Therefore, after the birth, she wrapped up the boy in a great fortune cookie which she left in the center of the monk's table and disappeared into the night.

One of the monks had not been fooled however. Old Master Toe, whose blindness was compensated for by his hearing had heard the child sucking his thumb before birth. This fact alone led Master Toe to believe that this child was to grow into a great man. So he arranged for the monks to adopt him. They would call him Caine and they would raise him thusly to avoid the pun.

After five years Caine had displayed qualities which made Master Toe realize that he had not been in error. The monks were experts at martial arts and for years Master Toe had been working on a new system of attack which his enfeebled bowels were no longer capable of. However the great long-windedness of young Caine made Master Toe realize, "If thy mouth be plugged, surely the wind will bloweth elsewhere."

The new system had come to Master Toe by accident. After a meal of Mexican refried beans, garbanzo and beer he had been set upon by a band of thieves. He had raised his leg to administer the "kick of the mule" when he broke wind with great force. The blast knocked down three of his adversaries and the odor caused them to succumb rapidly. There were no broken bones and their afflicted languidness made them

97

a cinch to tie up and begin to apply the Chinese smile torture to. This was a method of smiling inscrutably at the victim for hours until his mind broke. It did not work too well with Chinese, but with Italians and Armenians it was unbelievably cruel. Even so, the method was used successfully to put down the demonstrations among 309,457,651 or so peasants who labored to support the monastery. They demonstrated mainly for shorter hours, longer hair and white rice instead of brown.

Caine, who by now had become expert in snuffing candles with his toes and looking like the truly wise who appear truly dumbfounded, seemed to possess, perhaps as a result of his being a half-breed, an amazing set of bowels. All the monks had commented on such after meals. In fact it was Ky Tok himself who said, "The odor and strength of young Caine's fart reminds one of the hot east wind that blows across the garbage dump of Peking." And on another occasion, "If we could bottle young Caine"s flatulence we could become rich as Arabs."

And so it was done. Master Toe and Caine were given a special part of the monastery to work in. It was thick walled and down wind from the rest. They had their own kitchen to prepare special food for farting. After only a few years, this too was no longer enough for the thick walls were battered, the paint peeling and all the help had quit. Young Caine questioned Master Toe how any good could come if they destroyed so much and repulsed so many people. Master Toe replied, "From the most humble and unattractive foods, the most beautiful winds may come." To this young Caine only bowed his head, as he still understood no Chinese.

The training produced some magnificent results. Among them were these:

The Barking Spider: A short, self-contained burst of air repeated at regular intervals. It was most effective in dealing with large numbers of attackers. It enabled the defend-

ers to stun each one in turn while rotating
his backside in that man's direction.

The Whistling Wolf: A more prolonged blast that
slowly drove a man back and to his knees. This
worked best when there were fewer attacks as
it took a while to emit.

The Elephant Speaks: This was a tremendous
blast aimed at a single attacker which knocked him unconscious instantly.

To these three basic techniques, some variations were added, but more important a variety
of odors could be used with each technique:

The Hong Kong Horror: This was a heavy, foggy
smell which settled in slowly and gagged the
opponent.

The Singapore Stinck: This struck quickly and
crisply like a donkey and caused total sen-
sory disorientation on impact.

The Pittsburgh Patter: This was a surprise that
came in quickly and unexpectedly.

All were enough to knock out even the most
hardened sewer cleaner.
   Finally, after many years, Caine passed the
test that meant he must leave the monastery.
With but one blast he had obliterated the por-
celain parthenon, a toilet built for the horses
of Genghis Khan, and so large it supported his
whole herd at one time. So after dropping his
pants and sitting upon burning coals, young
Caine, now Master Caine, left to give to those
who deserved it their just desserts...
   Putt, putt, putt, we are now going to delve
into the subject of diet and how it relates to
the creation of farts. If you are interested
in increasing your tone, odor, length, endur-
ance, this may be of some assistance to you.
First of all, you should be reminded that one
should never overlook the familiar. I'm sure
you all remember those junior high jingles,
"Beans, beans, the musical fruit / The more you

eat the more you toot." There is, of course,
some validity in this despite the jejune nature
of the rhythm scheme. The late Addled Days,
whose extensive research brought her five husbands, four divorces, and unfortunately one
homicide, will be our guide in these matters,
putt, putt.

Putt, the dairy section, putt, is not especially good. It lacks bulk putt putt putt or
ferocity putt yet yogart putt creates a healthy
environment in the intestines putt. "It's a
weak bellows that blows ill." Putt, putt. However, the gastric juices are unable to quell
and acid pungencies of a stilton or limburger
and mild cheeses should be taken, putt, in mod-
eration and only, putt, before breakfast on
Tuesday...

PUTTPUTtPUttPutt putt...

And so having run out of air we have finally arrived at the end of this bountiful book. But no need to fret! Volume Two is already underway, and it is rapidly expanding! And when the new balloon is full, we at Melodious Publications can entice it to float your way. You may pop or poke it in any way you choose. Just send us your completed questionnaires, your anecdotes, *your fears*, and you will automatically be on our list... For the answer my friend, is indeed!, blowing in the wind!

Your friend,

E. Slove Prambles

the...

"Forgive us our gas-passings as we forgive those who pass gas among us." (41b:pg.380)

BIBLIOGRAPHY

2. Aristophanes.: *The Clouds*. (Translated by William Arrowsmith) University of Michigan Press, 1962. Pgs. 19-20, 35-36.

3. Asimov, Issac.: *Issac Asimov's Treasury of Humor*. Boston: Houghton Mifflin Co., 1971.

4. Aubrey, John.: *The Scandal and Credulities of John Aubrey*. New York: D. Appleton and Co., 1931. Pg. 16. (Edited by John Collier)

5. Barth, John.: *The Floating Opera*. Garden City, NY: Doubleday & Co., Inc., 1967.

6. Beckett, Samuel.: *I Can't Go On, I'll Go On: A Selection from Samuel Beckett's Work*. New York: Grove Press, 1976. Pg. 244.

6a. Berger, Thomas.: *Vital Parts*. New York: New American Library (Signet Books), 1970. Pg. 181.

7. Blyth, R.H.: *Oriental Humor*. Tokyo: The Hokuseido Press, 1968. Pgs. 129, 137, 159, 287, 292, 510, & 527.

9. Bourke, Capt. John G.: *Scatologic Rites of All Nations*. New York: American Anthropological Society, 1934. (Recently reprinted by Johnson Reproductions, New York)

10. Brand. "Fairy Mythology" and "Robin Goodfellow," *Popular Antiquities*. London, 1872. Pgs. 476 et. seq.

11. Burton, Richard F. (translator): *The Book of the Thousand Nights and a Night* (Arabian Nights). U.S.A.: Privately Printed by the Burton Club. Vol. 4 (Suppl.) Pgs. 178-9; Vol. 5 Pgs. 99, 135-7.

12. Castaneda, Carlos.: *A Separate Reality*. New York: Simon and Schuster, 1972.

13. Clemens, Samuel.: *1601 Conversation As It Was ... By the Social Fireside in the Time of the Tudors*. Hackensack, N.J.: Wehman Brothers, Inc., 1968.

14. Crantz.: *History of Greenland.* London, 1767. Vol. 1 Pg. 206.

15. Dali, Salvador.: *Diary of a Genius.* New York: Doubleday & Co., Inc., 1965. Pgs. 34-5, 53, & 59-60.

15b. Dali, Salvador.: *The Unspeakable Confessions of Salvador Dali,* (as told to Andre Parinaud). New York: William Morrow and Co., Inc., 1976.

16. Douglas, Norman.: *Some Limericks.* New York: Grove Press, 1967. Pgs. 38 & 69.

17. Feinberg, Leonard (Ed.): *Asian Laughter.* New York: Weatherhill Inc., 1971. Pg. 36.

18. Ferenczi, Sandor.: *Sex in Psycho-analysis.* New York: Dover, reprint 1956. Pgs. 114, 121 & 177.

19. Fiedler, Leslie.: *Being Busted.* New York: Stein and Day, 1969. Pg. 33.

20. Firestone, Clark B.: *Coasts of Illusion.* New York and London: Harper, 1924. Pgs. 107-8. All quotes from 35b.

20a. FitzGibbon, Theodora.: *The Food of the Western World.* New York: Quadrangle Press, 1976. Pg. 333.

21. Flower, Christopher.: "Coloration and Bottling of Crepitations: Developing New Areas in Fartology," *Journal of Fartology,* vol. 2, #3, 1971. Pgs. 23-34.

22. Gascoigne, George.: *The Complete Works of George Gascoigne.* (Ed. by John W. Cunliffe, II.) Cambridge: 1910. Pgs. 245-6.

23. Ginzberg, Ralph.: *An Unhurried View of Erotica.* New York: The Helmsman Press, 1958. Pgs. 76-82.

24. Hamilton, Edith.: *Mythology.* Boston: Little, Brown and Co., 1942. Pg. 43.

25. Hazlitt, W. Carew (Ed.): *Shakespeare Jest-Books*, vol. 2 & 3. New York 25, New York: Burt Franklin, 1864.

26. Josephson, Matthew.: *Edison*. New York: McGraw Hill, 1959. Pg. 23.

27. Lang, Andrew.: *Myth, Ritual and Religion*, vol. 2. London: 1887. Pg. 48. (Recently reprinted by AMS Press, N.Y.)

28. Lee, Jae Num.: *Swift and Scatological Satire*. Albuquerque, New Mexico: University of New Mexico Press, 1971.

29. Legman, G. (Ed.): *The Limerick*. New York: Brandywine Press, 1970. Pgs. 137-157.

30. Legman, G.: *The Rationale of the Dirty Joke* (Series 1 & 2). Vol. 1: New York: Grove Press, 1968. Vol 2: New Jersey: Breaking Point, Inc., 1975. Pgs. 858-890.

31. Montagu, Ashley.: *The Anatomy of Swearing*. New York: MacMillan Co., 1967.

32. Montaigne.: *The Complete Essays of Montaigne*. (Translated by Donald M. Frame) Stanford, California: Stanford University Press, 1965. Book 1, Chapter 21, Pgs. 72-3.

33. Nohaim, Jean & Caradec, F.: *Le Petomane* (*1857-1945*). (Translated by Warren Tute) Los Angeles: Sherbourne Press, Inc., 1967.

34. Pappas, T.: "An Eructologist Speaks," *Journal of Fartology*, vol. 4, #2, 1973. Pgs. 36-45.

35. Partridge, Eric.: *A Dictionary of Slang and Unconventional English*, 7th Edition. New York: McMillan Co., 1970. Pgs. 119, 267, 1129.

35a. Pellegrini, Angelo M.: *The Unprejudiced Palate*. New York: McMillan Co., 1948. Pgs. 39-40 & 196-198.

35b. Pliny.: *The Natural History of Pliny*. (Trans lated by John Bostock & H.T. Riley) London: Henry G. Bohn Press, 1855. Book 7, Chapter 2, Pgs. 131-2.

36. Promblés, E. Slove.: "A Tribute to 'Professor' Edward R. Eabos: Artist of Smell," *Journal of Fartology*, vol. 4, #2, 1973. Pgs. 47-64.

37. Promblés, E. Slove.: "What is Fartology?" *Journal of Fartology*, Vol. 1, #1, 1970. Pgs. 3-7.

38. *The Random House Dictionary of the English Language*. Jess Stern, Editor-in-Chief. New York: Random House, 1966.

39. Rabelais, Francois.: *Gargantua and Pantagruel*.

40. Rattray, Capt. R.S.: *Ashanti Law and Constitution*. London: Oxford University Press, 1956. Pgs. 372-373.

41. Rosebury, Theodor.: *Life on Man*. New York: The Viking Press, 1969.

41a. Sagan, Carl.: *The Cosmic Connection*. New York: Dell Publ. Co., Inc., 1975. Pgs. 149-150.

41b. Sherman, Allan.: *The Rape of A.P.E.* Chicago: The Playboy Press, 1973. Pgs. 378-380.

41e. Simon, Andre L. & Howe, Robin.: *A Dictionary of Gastronomy*. Woodstock, N.Y.: The Overlook Press, 1978.

42. Swift, Jonathan.: *Complete Poetical Works*.

43. Thompson, Stith.: *Motif-Index of Folk Literature*. Bloomington, Indiana: Indiana University Press, 1958.

44. Wallechinsky, David & Wallace, Irving & Amy.: *The Book of Lists*. New York: William Morrow & Co., Inc., 1977. Pg. 386.

45. Wilson, Edward O.: "Pheromones," *Scientific American*. May, 1963.
46. Wilson, Robert Anton.: *Forbidden Words*. Chicago: Playboy Press, 1972. Pgs. 111-2.
47. Zall, P.M. (Ed.): *A Hundred Merry Tales and Other English Jestbooks of the Fifteenth and Sixteenth Centuries*. University of Nebraska Press, 1963. Pg. 269.

DO NOT TURN THE PAGE UNTIL YOU HAVE DECIDED
WHICH PERSON YOU REALLY ARE ! ! !

1. THE VAIN PERSON
2. THE AMIABLE PERSON
3. THE PROUD PERSON
4. THE SHY PERSON
5. THE IMPUDENT PERSON
6. THE SCIENTIFIC PERSON
7. THE NERVOUS PERSON
8. THE HONEST PERSON
9. THE DISHONEST PERSON
10. THE UNFORTUNATE PERSON
11. THE FOOLISH PERSON
12. THE THRIFTY PERSON
13. THE ANTI-SOCIAL PERSON
14. THE STRATEGIC PERSON
15. THE SADISTIC PERSON
16. THE INTELLECTUAL PERSON
17. THE ATHLETIC PERSON
18. THE MISERABLE PERSON
19. THE SENSITIVE PERSON

1. One who loves the smell of his own farts.

2. One who loves the smell of other people's farts.

3. One who thinks his farts are exceptionally fine.

4. One who releases silent farts and then blushes.

5. One who boldly farts out loud and then laughs.

6. One who farts regularly, but is truly concerned with pollution.

7. One who stops in the middle of a fart.

8. One who admits he farted but offers a good medical reason.

9. One who farts and then blames the dog.

10. One who tries awfully hard to fart but shits instead.

11. One who suppresses a fart for hours and hours.

12. One who always has several farts to spare.

13. One who excuses himself and then leaves the room to fart.

14. One who conceals his fart....???

15. One who farts in bed and then fluffs up the covers.

16. One who can determine from the smell of a fart what you had for dinner.

17. One who farts with the sli....???

18. One who would truly love to but can't fart at all.

19. One who farts and then starts crying.

THE MELODIOUS QUESTIONNAIRE

1. Age:
2. Sex:
3. Nationality:
4. Fluently spoken languages:
5. What kind of person did you claim to be?
6. Do you feel that this kind of psychological testing is accurate?
7. How would you improve it?
8. Would you join a religion that venerated the fart?
9. If yes, a) What kind of ceremonies would you expect?

   b) What costume should everyone wear?

   c) Should the services be in Latin?
10. What amusing/tragic experiences have you had that dealt with farts and/or farting?
11. How did you deal with the situation?
12. If Catholic, did you confess it?
13. What stories have you heard from your friends and their acquaintances?
14. What is your favorite fart joke?
15. Where did you hear it?
16. Do you name your farts?
17. If so, what do you name them?
18. What color are your farts?
19. Are everybody's the same color? Explain:
20. What is the most a fart can weigh?
21. What is the least?
22. Are your farts translucent?

23. What are their shapes?

24. Do they rise or fall?

25. Do they bounce?

26. Describe their trajectories:

27. Do you save them?

28. If so, what method of preservation do you practice?

29. Do your farts conduct electricity?

30. What did you like best about my book?

31. What did you like the least?

32. How would you have done it?

33. Would you like to learn more about the Science of Fartology?

34. If so, send in the above data. Word on how to obtain the results and interpretations will be forwarded to you as soon as all the data is in and it is thoroughly studied.

Thank you for filling out my questionnaire.

Send your questionnaire answers to Melodious Publications, POB 343, Brockport, New York, 14420. But remember: *"All correspondence sent to Melodious Publications will be treated as unconditionally assigned for publication. Upon receipt, these items will become the exclusive property of Melodious Publications and as such are subject to Melodious Publications' unrestricted right to edit and comment editorially and artistically."*

I, _____, agree to the above conditions and am willing to allow Melodious Publications do whatever they may with whatever I am sending them. I understand that neither my name nor address will be revealed unless I emphatically request it in an attached letter.

Signed: _____

Date: _____

P.S.   *Would you like to be on the record, soon to be recorded? If so, send demo tapes to Melodious Recordings, c/o Melodious Publications. Tapes will not be returned unless a self-addressed stamped envelope is enclosed.*

Melodius Publications
P.O. Box 343, Brockport, NY 14420

Please send me _____ copies of **FEE, FIE, FOE, FUM** @ 5.95 each, postage paid. (NYS residents add 42¢ sales tax for each book ordered.)

☐ Send _____ copies as a gift to names and addresses attached.

☐ Please enclose gift cards.

Mail check or money order payable to Melodious Publications.

Name _____

Address _____

_____

T-SHIRTS!

Please send me _____ T-Shirts with the cover of **FEE, FIE, FOE, FUM** on the front of it for only $3.98 each, postage paid. (NYS residents add 28¢ sales tax for each shirt ordered.)

☐ Send _____ shirts as a gift to names and addresses attached. Don't forget to indicate sizes!

☐ Please enclose gift cards.

Make check or money order payable to Melodious Publications.

Name _____

Address _____

_____

Size: small ☐   medium ☐   large ☐   X-large ☐